Conscience of a Profession:

HOWARD SWAN
Choral
Director
and Teacher

Charles Fowler, Editor

Editorial Advisors:
Rosemary Heffley
and Sally Schott

Editorial Research:
Linda Allen Anderson
Donna Dutton
Ruth Whitlock

HINSHAW MUSIC, INC.
CHAPEL HILL, NORTH CAROLINA 27514

Library of Congress Card Number 87-80370
ISBN 0-937276-07-3

Printed in the United States of America

Contents

Introduction

There isn't a choral conductor alive who doesn't have something to learn from Howard Swan about the choral craft—or its passengers.

He knows so much about what makes a conductor good and a chorus great—and how to get there from here—that it's absolutely mystifying why both things don't happen more often.

If you're interested in being a better conductor—or even a better person—buy the book! If you don't notice an immediate improvement, you'll at least know where the trouble lies.

Robert Shaw
Atlanta, Georgia
February 13, 1987

Preface/Acknowledgements

To bestow the title "conscience of his profession" on Howard Swan is to acknowledge his pervasive influence on choral music during his five decades of service. This compilation of his teachings—drawn from representative lectures, articles, interviews, conversations and rehearsals—displays his unique style of communication. His thoughts reveal the quality of the person and provide concrete testimony as to the reasons so many have learned from him and been inspired by him.

The material that has been assembled here cuts a wide swath across the fifty years Dr. Swan has been an active force in the world of choral music. His philosophical and professional viewpoints have remained reassuringly consistent throughout that span. Thus, the articles within each category are placed in chronological order. Approximately half the material is appearing in print for the first time; the remainder is reprinted from professional journals and other sources. Some changes in punctuation have been made to make more readable the material that was originally composed for oral delivery. A number of published and unpublished pieces are excerpted with quotations placed on the left hand side of the pages. Quotations on the right hand side of the pages are quotes extracted from the adjacent articles to highlight specific points. An appendix provides a listing of the sources as well as other writings pertaining to Dr. Swan.

This volume represents a labor borne of respect and affection. In the late 1970's, Ruth Whitlock, a former Occidental College student of Dr. Swan's and now a faculty member at Texas Christian University, first approached Mrs. Swan and then Dr. Swan: could she collect his "papers" and facilitate their publication? His positive response led her to enlist the aid of Californians Linda Anderson and Donna Dutton, also former Swan students at Occidental College.

Perhaps it is a sign of Dr. Swan's magnanimity that the project soon became a joint effort of people in two states—California and Texas. Dr. Swan's distinctive service as a three-time All-State Choir clinician and speaker for both the 1977 and 1985 Texas Music Educators Association Symposia enabled that state's choral directors and performers to experience his humanity, artistry and wisdom firsthand. Having been privileged to work with Dr. Swan while serving as state officers of TMEA and TCDA, Sally Schott and Rosemary Heffley were honored to accept fellow Texan Whitlock's invitation to become a part of the project.

At the national MENC Convention in March, 1986, the California contingent met with the Texas connection and Dr. and Mrs. Swan for an initial exchange of manuscripts. Since that time a number of other people have given assistance. Recognition must be given to the special contributions of Sue Bradle, Dede Duson, Lois Land, to members of Hinshaw Music Company, particularly Roberta Marchese, and to all of the participants for the many hours they have willingly given. This is truly a concerted effort, guided by the notion that Dr. Swan's positive and professional influence will continue to reverberate for generations to come.—*Ed*.

Foreword

One day when I was a little girl, one of my mother's friends pointed out to me that my grandfather was listed in that year's edition of *Who's Who in America*. She must have perceived my puzzlement, for she then asked me how I felt. I replied naively though honestly that I never thought of Howard Swan as a well-known choral conductor, but just as my grandfather. I still remember that day's revelation vividly, for although I had attended Occidental Glee Club concerts I had never identified Grandpa with his profession: choral conducting was what he *did*, not what he *was*.

Howard Swan *is* a choral conductor; he is also a husband, father, grandfather, and friend. His professional and personal lives have always been inextricably intertwined. During the too few times I worked with him as his student, I learned rapidly how very important his relationships with family and friends are to his work. But as I grew older, I began to realize how much the essence of his vocation is also very much a part of his personal life. The articles in this book tell much about music and conducting—yet just as much about the human being who wrote them.

As an artist/musician, what Hawthorne would have called a true "Artist of the Beautiful," my grandfather possesses an intuitive recognition of, and love for, beauty. His desire both to create the beautiful and to help others do so is predominant in his personality. How disturbed he becomes when ugliness rears its spirit-destroying head! Often during the late sixties and early eventies, I heard him bemoan various fashion trends on the Occidental campus: most objectionable were his students' bare feet. "How can I teach the beauty of Bach while staring at fifteen-odd pairs of dirty feet?" he would grumble.

One does not, however, have to attend his classes to realize his appreciation of the beautiful. I remember one summer when he and my grandmother were visiting my family in the San Francisco Bay Area. On a ferry trip across the Bay, he grabbed my arm and pointed to the Golden Gate Bridge, glistening in the setting sun. "Look at that grace!" he exclaimed. "doesn't that remind you of a ballet dancer?" His excitement over the form and sweep of the bridge opened up to me a world of metaphor and imagery; since then I have been able to think of the bridge only in his way.

Clearly, Grandpa is an artist/poet/musician. As with all good choral conductors, however, teaching is as much a part of him as is his music. How excited he gets when showing a student a new way to interpret a phrase! How he enjoys discussing ideas with people of any age! I recall on visit I made to him and my grandmother when I was about seven: he and I spent a good hour after dinner earnestly discussing the novel I was going to write as soon as I got home. Although the subject of my novel was certainly not intellectual (I think it was about the adventures of a girl and her horse), Grandpa was seriously interested in the plot, characters, and structure of my book, asking probing questions while warmly encouraging my fledgling efforts. Years followed. Dinner table conversations with his grandchildren became more controversial and issue-oriented. . . . Nevertheless, Grandpa continued to be supportive; however, while he never minded being disagreed with, he found intellectual laziness unacceptable and always demanded of us hard, critical thinking and focused, substantiated arguments.

To my deep regret, given problems of time and distance, I will probably never study music with Howard Swan. Even so, in a very real sense, my cousins, my siblings, and I have always been his students. Everything that he is as a conductor—whether in the rehearsal hall or on stage—he is as a grandfather. He is artist, scholar, teacher, and friend—to all who know him, either professionally or personally.

Ann Schwarberg Gaillard
Dallas, Texas
February, 1987

1

Howard Swan:
The Man and
His Philosophy

Howard Swan

Howard Swan's remarkable professional career spans nearly sixty years. Well-known as one of the most dynamic forces in twentieth century choral music, this optimistic realist, whose demeanor re-diates a love for choral music and a faith in his fellow man, has enriched the lives of all those who have come into contact with him. His phenomenal performances, powerful personality, positive philosophy, proven perspicacity, pedagogical patience, and persistent profession-alism have had a profound effect on the complexion of the choral art.

Born in Denver, Colorado, on March 29, 1906, Howard Shelton Swan moved to southern California with his family of amateur musicians in 1912. His father, chairman of the mathematics department of Los Angeles High School and later vice-principal of Fairfax High School, was a singer who occasionally conducted a church choir. Howard's mother played the piano, and Howard and his sister and two brothers all sang. Howard also studied the violin.

At Hollywood High School, he sang in the glee club and performed in operettas under the guidance of the first teacher to exert a strong influence on his musical education, music department chairman Edna Ames. Later he would study with Father Finn, the great conductor of boys' choirs, John Finley Williamson, founder of the Westminster Choir College, and F. Melius Christiansen, director of the famed St. Olaf College Choir.

Intending that music be an avocation, Howard enrolled at Pomona College as a history major. He made the Glee Club as a freshman and sang Robin Hood in the operetta. In 1924, as a sophomore, he met a lovely freshman named Katherine Smith. Even though she transferred two years later to the University of California, Berkeley, where she earned a degree, the romance persisted and the young couple were married in Bridges Hall in December, 1929, with Joseph Clokey, college organist, at the console. The Swans now have two sons, David and Robert, a daughter, Katherine Elizabeth Schwarberg, and eight grandchildren.

In 1928 Howard Swan earned a B.A. degree in history, with a minor in political science from Pomona College. A fifth year there permitted him to qualify for a state teacher's credential in social studies. During that year, Professor Ralph Lyman took sabbatical leave, and Howard was asked to conduct the glee club. Howard also was hired as

3

tenor soloist at First Methodist Church of Hollywood and at the B'nai B'rith (Wilshire Boulevard) Temple.

Shortly after he began his first teaching position in social studies at Eagle Rock High School, Mr. Swan became the tenor soloist at Immanuel Presbyterian Church. He also sang on the Bob Burns and Raymond Paige radio shows and in several motion pictures, including "Devil's Island" with Ronald Coleman and "Northwest Mounted Police" with Nelson Eddy. In addition he gained experience in madrigal singing and an interest in the a cappella movement through performing in John Smallman's quartet, the Tudor Singers.

When the Eagle Rock authorities learned that he had done some conducting in college, they asked Mr. Swan to take over their boys' glee club. The next year he requested permission from the Eagle Rock principal, Helen Babson, to establish an a cappella choir similar to Ida Bach's Fremont High School A Cappella Choir, the only one in Los Angeles in 1932. Helen answered, "Well, I don't know what it is; I don't know how to spell it, but if you'd like it, you may have one." Soon Eagle Rock High School had two a cappella choirs and then three. With Louis Curtis, music supervisor for the Los Angeles School District, Howard organized the first a cappella festival to be held in southern California.

In 1933 Howard Swan lost his voice to a sudden paralysis of the vocal cords. As a consequence of this devastating occurrence, diagnosed years later as a viral infection and corrected surgically in 1971, he was forced to abandon solo singing in favor of choral conducting. Thus began his ten-year association with Highland Park Presbyterian Church as director of music.

From 1934 to 1937 he continued his duties at Eagle Rock High School and began conducting the Men's and Women's Glee Clubs at Occidental College. In 1937, he was hired full-time at Occidental to continue his choral work, teach some classes, and direct the activities of Thorne Hall. He remained on the Occidental College faculty until 1971, becoming music department chairman in 1948 and serving in that capacity for twenty years. He earned an M.A. degree in Psychology from Claremont College in 1941 and an Honorary Doctorate in Music from Pomona College in 1959. He received a Ford Foundation Fellowship in 1962 as well as a Rockefeller grant to study conducting in Europe.

Under Dr. Swan's direction, the Occidental Glee Clubs flourished. He developed peerless choirs which toured the United States, recorded the Brahms' *Alto Rhapsody* and *Schicksalslied* with Bruno Walter and the Columbia Symphony Orchestra in 1961, gained international acclaim during a 1965 European tour under the auspices of the U.S. State Department, and won awards at the prestigious Interna-

4

tional Eisteddfod Competition held in Llangollen, North Wales, in 1968.

He contributed twenty years of distinguished service (1940–1960) as Director of Music at Pasadena Presbyterian Church, which boasted six choirs, its own radio station, and a house on Balboa Island where he regularly conducted choir camps.

A founding member of both the Southern California Vocal Association (1938) and the Choral Conductor's Guild (President, 1944–45 and 1952–53), he also served the American Choral Directors' Association from 1964 to 1967 as the first Western Division President. He is a member of Pi Kappa Lambda and has been elected to honorary life membership in Phi Mu Alpha Sinfonia, CCG, SCVA, and ACDA.

Dr. Swan's book, *Music in the Southwest: 1825–1950*, was published in 1952. He is a co-author of *Choral Music—A Symposium*, published in 1973, and a contributor ("Music in Los Angeles") to the new sixth edition of *Grove's Dictionary of Music and Musicians*. In addition, he has written for publications of the Book Club of California and has penned numerous articles for *The Quarterly Journal* of the

Katherine and Howard Swan, 1985

Huntington Library, the *Diapason*, *The Journal of Choral Conductors' Guild* of California, the *Southern California Vocal Association Newsletter* and *The Choral Journal* of the American Choral Directors' Association. His biography appears in *Who's Who in America*.

Dr. Swan has been a personal mentor for many artists, including pianist John Browning and conductor Robert Shaw. He has conducted countless honor choirs and all-state choruses, including performances for both National and Division Conventions of the Music Educators' National Conference. He has served as a lecturer/clinician at more than fifty colleges and universities in the U.S. and Canada, at numerous professional meetings, and at some of this country's most prestigious summer choral institutes.

From 1971 to 1977, Dr. Swan served as Coordinator of Graduate Music Studies at California State University, Fullerton, where he also organized the University Chorale, a 100-voice choir composed of undergraduate and graduate students, faculty members, former students, son Dave and daughter-in-law Helen, and many choral conductors who eagerly flocked to Fullerton once a week from all over southern California to learn from the master.

In 1977, he was presented an Honorary Doctorate in Humanities by Westminster Choir College. Since 1978 he has served as a Lecturer in Choral Music at University of California, Irvine, and in 1986 he was presented with an honorary doctorate by Occidental College.

Howard and Katherine Swan now live at beautiful Presbyterian Regents Point in Irvine, where he conducts a volunteer chorus composed of the residents.

Reflections of an Optimistic Realist

Howard Swan prepared this address for delivery at the National Convention of the American Choral Directors Association in San Antonio on March 14, 1987. This convention was dedicated to Howard Swan.

Why is it that so often these days we accept without any argument a philosophy or a point of view which basically is unhappy in its thought and content? Isn't it a fact that with almost every kind of activity criticism must be negative to have value and reality? On the other hand, evidence which is both encouraging and positive often is greeted with doubt or even suspicion. Do we honestly believe that to be on the safe side one always should equate pessimism with reality?

This situation often creates an interesting and somewhat humorous paradox. We wonder about the motives of that rare person who attempts to find good in a particular circumstances—who digs about hoping to discover elements of truth which also possess the virtues of happiness and good cheer. Yet at the same time we disagree with this philosophy, we find ourselves wishing to draw more closely to the individual whose speech and actions obviously are those of an optimist.

I suppose that we can agree that the times in which we live are partially responsible for the development of a pessimistic spirit—a kind of credo which affects adversely almost everyone. When we consider the worlds of government, finance, politics and education, we are aware that many of our leaders have lost their creditability and our confidence. On all sides we see the results of an alarming increase in terrorism and violent crimes of every description. Even more frightening is the knowledge that we are living with a fear of eventual destruction, whether such is to be accomplished by nuclear or atomic device or with the use of drugs which are capable of exterminating vast segments of the population. Our cultural arts: painting, literature, motion pictures, the theatre, T.V. and some musical performances too often mirror this pessimistic state of affairs. But, if one voices an objection to the tastelessness and impropriety found in some particular presentation, such is met with the harsh reply that these agencies have the responsibility to inform all of us how contemporary society thinks, acts and lives.

While some geographical areas in America have been able to avoid adversity, all of us recognize that our musical world has had its share of gloom and despair. Whenever school choral conductors gather in groups of three or three hundred, their conversation and the atmosphere it engenders is one of pessimism. Some possible examples are:

"I hear that a school district over on the west side has presented pink slips to all of their music teachers." From California: "So our students will be required to enroll for a year of foreign language *or* visual or performing arts. And the language is needed for their college or university entrance. Guess my choir will continue to meet at 6:30 every morning." From Texas: "How can we plan for a year's program in music if students must drop the class because of failing another course?" "Ron Smith says that Bill Jones has gone to the Rancho Grande Vista City Schools. He won't last the year out with that crusty superintendent and his tightwad school board."

This discussion continues with considerable disagreement concerning a cause for the present state of affairs. It is the fault of the legislature or the antipathy of the general public towards education. It is the declining birthrate which has led to the closing of many schools or the negative influence of some TV programs. On and on it goes. Nor is this bitter attitude found only among school musicians. Those who have church positions speak of ministers who know nothing of a "real" program for music and worship and choirs who resent being asked to do anything which either is new or a departure from traditional rehearsal techniques. Finally, those who conduct community or semi-professional choruses add their collective voice of despair. It goes like this: "We don't see how we can continue in business now that our budget has been cut so drastically by our board . . . or by our corporate sponsors . . . or by government agencies." So the gloomy talk continues whether the discussion centers about music education, music in the church or a musical activity which depends upon community aid.

Optimistic and pessimistic viewpoints have long been a source for acclaim, contempt, or humor depending upon the issue. Voltaire had Candide speak these words: "Optimism is a mania for maintaining that all is well when things are going badly."[1] Perhaps one agrees with the humor of James Branch Cabell when he asserts that "the optimist proclaims that we live in the best of all possible worlds, and the pessimist fears that this is true."[2] And an old saying now appears in these four lines of verse:

Twixt the optimist and pessimist
The difference is droll;
The optimist sees the doughnut
But the pessimist sees the hole.[3]

[1] Francois Marie Arout Voltaire, *Candide*. John Bartlett, Ed. *Familiar Quotations* 14th ed. (Boston: Little, Brown and Co., 1968) p. 417.
[2] James Branch Cabell, *The Silver Stallion* Ch. 26. John Bartlett, ed. *Familiar Quotations* p. 417.
[3] McLandburgh Wilson, *Optimist and pessimist*, John Bartlett, ed. *Familiar Quotations* p. 943.

But now we should become somewhat more serious and work with these useful definitions which appear in the American Heritage Dictionary. Here, pessimism is said to be "a tendency to take the gloomiest possible view of a situation." And again, "the doctrine or belief that this is the worst of all possible worlds and that all things ultimately tend towards evil." Now—what of optimism? "A tendency or disposition to expect the best possible outcome or to dwell upon the most hopeful aspects of a situation." And a second: "The doctrine, asserted by Leibnitz, that our world is the best of all possible worlds."

"A realist," says our authority, "is one who is inclined to literal truth and pragmatism." "Reality is genuine and authentic, not artificial or spurious."[4]

As so often happens my study of dictionary and thesaurus resulted in my learning a word, pertinent to this commentary, which I had never heard before. The term is *meliorist*—and its meaning, "one who believes that society has an innate tendency toward improvement and that this tendency may be furthered through conscious human effort."[5] I like that one!

I expect that all of us would disagree with Herr Leibnitz when he writes optimistically that "this is the best of all possible worlds." In what ways does the world of music fail to meet expectations? Most of us probably are critical of inadequate compensation; we don't receive enough for the many responsibilities we are asked to assume. A second source for caustic criticism is the incongruity of class schedules. We may be required to teach subjects other than music or to conduct a band rather than a chorus. College and university staff members will count themselves fortunate to be placed in a tenure track although they are fearful in realizing that there are but few institutions which make allowances for performances in place of publication or the study for an advanced degree. Still another reason for our dissatisfaction can be the person or persons with whom we work. He or she may be a minister, dean, the chairperson of a finance committee, or a surfaced custodian. We don't like them because of personal idiosyncrasies or their lack of cooperation or just because they get in the way of what we are trying to do.

If time permitted we could formulate an extensive list of reasons why we dislike and sometimes even despise our work. Now and then we may wonder if we are becoming candidates for a real burnout. Our plans for recruitment bring no tenors—we are sick and tired of singing Christmas carols each year for sixteen service clubs—too much time is wasted in maintaining order in the rehearsals, and so on. In many

---

[4] *American Heritage Dictionary of the English Language* (New York: American Heritage Publishing Company. 1969).
[5] Ibid.

Only the best is good enough.—Address, Western Division convention of the Choral Directors Association, Pasadena, California, 1982.

instances our grievances are legitimate, but there seems to be no sure way by which all difficulties can be made to disappear.

However—I suggest that perhaps many of us have forgotten how and why it was that we made the choice of choral music as a profession. Surely it was not for the financial rewards, important though these may be. Realistic satisfaction and exciting fulfillment for all of us comes about when there is an increasing involvement with music as a great and wonderful art. We cannot begin to know all that music has to give until first we master those technical, expressional and communicative elements which constitute the musical experience.

I have been reading again some of the letters written by several of our greatest musicians of past years. These were selected by Hans Gal, who was himself a superb performer and composer. He makes these perceptive comments concerning the letters:

> It is hardly possible to read the records of great musicians' lives as they emerge from their own expressions of thought, without being struck by the preponderance of tragedy, of frustration, of self-sacrifice revealed in such documents: the fate of those who died as it were by the wayside, such as Mozart, Chopin, Weber (and Bartok's name could be added here), or had to live in obscurity such as Bach, Schubert, Wolf, or achieved right at the end of their lives of untold toil and drudgery a haphazard recognition by a small minority, such as Berlioz or Bruckner. It looks as if the inevitable corollary of greatness were martyrdom. . . . Any conclusion, however, would be misleading without due consideration of an essential redeeming feature: the indescribable bliss the artist finds in his work as the highest fulfillment of his destiny. Creating is the aim and end of the artist's instinct. His struggles and sufferings are but passing clouds; the reality is his work, . . . [6]

If technical artistry is to be an important goal for a choral director, how does one begin? A discussion concerning all of the techniques needed for recreating a score could fill a book or furnish enough information to service half a hundred workshops. But, regardless of age or experience, one always must cultivate early and late the ability to *hear*. The practice of this skill should never end. Improvement will follow in due course, but very seldom will the conductor develop the ability to hear everything that is happening in the rehearsal or performance. Also, the wise director will see to it that the singers become proficient with their ability to listen. I trust that the results of such rigorous practice will be much happier than was true of the man who always had wanted to conduct an orchestra. According to the story, he made a fortune and hired a group of players. However, his instrumentation was queer indeed: thirty-nine strings and one drummer. As you might expect, the rehearsal went badly because of the ignorance of the so-called conductor. At their first break many of the players were for

---

[6] Hans Gal, *The Musicians World* (New York: Arco Publishing Co., Inc. 1966) p. 448

walking out in disgust. But others said "He has paid us quite well—give him another chance—things are bound to improve." So they returned to their rehearsal but all went from bad to worse. The drummer finally became so angry that he began to beat his drums in a wild rage. Whereupon the conductor stopped the players, glared around the room and shouted "Who did that!"

In addition to the ability to listen, what are other skills which must be considered as basic for every conductor who works both for integrity and distinction? I list these without comment: the ability to ascertain a proper tempo for every piece, and do not hold back from experimentation. Teach for a special in-tune-ness from the chorus. Develop a sensitivity to inner rhythms and an opportunity to work with the voices. May the next decade see several additions to our present All-American unanimity towards "Yawn-sigh." May we gain the wisdom to make excellent choices of quality literature. I am pleased to note that those who are conscientious in this respect are aware that there is a vast difference in standards both for the so-called "classical" compositions and for entertainment music as well.

Working with and achieving a mastery of the technical and expressional factors in choral music develops a comforting self-confidence for the choral conductor. In turn, such assurance helps in understanding how one's professional life can be exciting and challenging without the necessity for egotistical pretense and affectation.

But this is not all. You and I are fortunate to live in a familiar world of color and sound, of form-shape, perspective and balance, factors which relate to charm and grace, order and beauty. At this moment you are able to be sensitive to all which you see and hear and feel if you wish it; every passing day can find you in a world which is new and different. All that is necessary is that you allow the artistic desire which has been within you to be creatively fulfilled, not just once but many times.

To realize fully our potential, we should accept the premise that every form of artistic expression needs other human beings who are willing with us to perceive and appreciate what we are trying to say, to sing, or to do. Do you know these meaningful two lines? The woods would be very silent if only those birds sang who sing the best. Because of mutual need there arise so many opportunities to experience the finest in human relationships. We learn to sympathize with failure and rejoice with success. One laughs with but not at others. Possessed by a shared understanding of the human spirit, people can become persons. All of this happens if those who are in charge desire to have it so.

Bruno Walter, the eminent and beloved symphonic conductor, ends his autobiography with these words: "There flows from music irrespective of its everchanging emotional expression an unchanging

11

message of comfort. . . . Music as an element has an optimistic quality and I believe that therein lies the source of my innate optimism. . . . I have been vouchsafed the grace to be a servant of music. It has been a beacon on my way and has kept me in the direction towards which I have been striving—darkly when I was a child, consciously later. There lie my hope and my confidence."[7]

How many of us think of music as a wondrous magic link with God—taking sometimes the place of prayer when words have failed us 'neath the weight of care. Music which knows no race nor creed—but gives to all according to their need.
And—that is what it's all about.

---

[7] Bruno Walter, *Theme and Variations* (New York: Alfred A. Knopf, 1947) p. 344.

2
Credo:
The Church
Musician

A favorite quote of Dr. Swan's:

One doesn't build upon hatred. One doesn't build upon discouragement, but upon love. Love sustains the artist. Love wants to rise, not to be held down by anything base. Nothing is more gentle than love, nothing stronger, nothing higher, nothing more pleasant, nothing more complete, nothing better in heaven or on earth— because love is born of God and cannot rest other than in God above all living beings. He who loves, flies, runs, and rejoices. He is free and nothing holds him back.

Henri Matisse

14

The Creed of a Chorister

*Director of Music at Pasadena Presbyterian Church for many years, Swan deliv-
ered this address at Choir Recognition Day, June 10, 1945. Shared again at a
church service in Honolulu, Hawaii in September of 1981.*

From earliest times as men and women have accepted membership in an organization they have endeavored to express their hopes for
the future and their belief in the present in a statement of faith and
purpose. We call such a statement a creed. When you boys become
members of the Cubs or the Scouts, as the girls may join the Campfire
Girls or the Girl Scout organization, you subscribe to a set of principles which endeavors to define the beliefs of the group. You repeat "A
Scout is helpful, a Scout is loyal, or a Scout is reverent" and so on,
and what is meant is that all who become Boy Scouts believe that it is
a very good thing for a fellow to be helpful, to be loyal, and to be reverent.

The Christian Church, very early in its history, felt the necessity
for a creed of some sort to which its members could agree and in their
agreement might find themselves a body of believers set apart from the
pagan world. So it was that in the fourth century after Christ, the
Council of Nicea formulated a creed which is said or sung today in
many Christian churches sixteen hundred years after it was first accepted. The Apostles Creed, familiar to many of us, was derived for
the Nicene Creed and in many respects is similar to it in wording and
content.

There will always be times when men and women will find it necessary to unite themselves in support of a set of principles—in a statement of their beliefs to which they subscribe with enthusiasm. This is
true of the members of a church choir. What, then, are the beliefs concerning our responsibilities which unite us in a common purpose?
What should be the creed for a chorister?

I suggest three statements of purpose which can be accepted by
those who give service to their church with their music:

First, as a chorister one believes in the power of great music.
Such music often has been inspired in its composition. One understands that song sometimes can do much towards working a vital
transformation in the lives of men. As a singer I must use all my talent:
mind, voice and emotion to give to this music a careful, devout,

*One understands that song
sometimes can do much
towards working a vital
transformation in the lives of
men.*

thoughtful interpretation. And I accept the fact that this takes rehearsal.

Secondly, as a chorister I am loyal both to my director and to the other singers in the choir. I will rejoice in their successes and encourage them when they fail. I understand that there is no place for jealousy of others. I know that other singers like myself have their faults and shortcomings. They can make mistakes; they will have periods of discouragement. However, I must believe that these friends are trying as I am to be of service to the cause of Christ wherever His name is known. As a chorister I must believe in and appreciate the inherent goodness of those who serve with me in the choir.

Finally, I believe in my church. I accept the way of life taught and lived by Jesus Christ. I cannot underestimate the importance of serving others. I accept wholeheartedly the teaching that love for my fellows is the greatest thing in the world. Because I love and believe in my church, I understand that the services of public worship are important and that my music can contribute to each one of them. Therefore, I will always be reverent in the house of God. As I lead others in worship, as I sing, as I petition or praise my God, I will endeavor to make more purposeful and helpful everything which I do.

To love great music, to believe in and appreciate my fellow singers, and to serve Jesus Christ with a sincere devotion—these are three great principles embodied in the creed of a chorister. It is with the acceptance of these articles of faith that our music program will continue to grow. Not only will this happen with numbers of singers and their activities but with the knowledge that our service is enriched because the spirit of Christ is present in our hearts and is working through our lives.

Relationships Between Choirmaster and Clergyman

Lecture delivered to ministers, music ministers, and laymen at Southern California Theological Seminary on October 12, 1960. Swan facetiously entitled it "The Great Debate," "A New Approach to Harmony," and "The War Department in the Jet Age" before seriously settling on the present title.

I am assuming that in this audience there are representatives of three groups who should have a strong interest in the nature and practice of a proper program of church music. First, there are those of you who are now, or who plan to become, ministers of the gospel. Some of you are directly responsible for the character of the music in your churches; you are directors of music, ministers of music, organists; or you are blessed with some such title. Finally, I hope that we have some interested laymen listening in on the discussion.

I would like to talk with you about some of the problems which are very pertinent to music as we hear it in the church. My thesis is this: Many of these problems are caused by a certain amount of ignorance, misunderstanding and complacency on the part of those who should be most vitally concerned—the minister and the choirmaster. Often, they do not understand the problem, nor do they understand each other.

Perhaps you noticed that no title was announced for what I might have to say. In a facetious mood and in keeping with the contemporary theme we might term it "The Great Debate." Because church music departments, whether cynically or truthfully, are sometimes called "The War Department," this essay might be titled "The War Department In The Jet Age." Or in a musical vein, how about this—"A New Approach to Harmony"? Speaking seriously, however, we had better stay with the forthright statement—"Relationships Between Choirmaster and Clergyman."

I wonder if it is necessary to debate the fact that music does aid in the experience of worship. You will remember that the Hebrews set apart a group of singers and instrumentalists who were charged with a solemn responsibility for music in the temple services. The Greeks gave to music a position of great honor in their religious observances. Following the exhortation of St. Paul to teach and to admonish with psalms, hymns, and spiritual songs, the first Christians and their des-

For approximately sixteen centuries following the birth of Christ, that music which was of high artistic standards, which called upon professional composers for its creation and skilled choristers for its interpretation—this was the music used in the service of the Christian church.

cendants who developed a universal church during the middle ages thought of music as a vital element in worship. The priest sang the mass; he did not recite it. Choir singers were enrolled in schools designed to prepare them for their sacred calling. For approximately sixteen centuries following the birth of Christ, that music which was of high artistic standards, which called upon professional composers for its creation and skilled choristers for its interpretation—this was the music used in the service of the Christian church.

Nor was this high regard for music confined to the early church. The many hymn texts which came from the pen of Martin Luther testify to the belief of this great Protestant in the power of religious song. In 16th century England, John Merbecke was instructed to take the then new Book of Common Prayer and give it a musical setting of "a note to each syllable." A few years later the revised prayer book carried explicit instructions that after the sermon "the choir shall sing an anthem."

As Protestantism became a separatist movement, and as non-liturgical denominations grew in power—sacred music, at least, that part which was influenced by this new kind of worship practice, unfortunately became both less important in effectiveness and less artistic in achievement. The dull, stodgy hymn which was lined out in a Scotch kirk or Puritan meeting house gave little impetus to the creation of that which we might call *beauty* in worship. It was not until Isaac Watts and the Wesleys appeared on the scene that hymnody regained the spontaneity and the joy that was its birthright.

Historically speaking, some of the change in the character and performance of sacred music was a direct result of the shift from a liturgical to a freer form of public worship. For hundreds of years the manner in which a Christian publicly practiced his religious responsibilities had been prescribed, unalterable and unquestioned. A Theology which supposedly was infallible was clothed in a text which was traditional, dignified and beautiful. Even more important—the ritual itself had developed as a preparation for the great central act which was a constant reminder of Christ's Last Supper—whether the rite was believed to contain miraculous elements or was highly regarded because of its commemorative aspects. Thus, in the liturgical church, a composer, while limited in the choice of text, was permitted to exercise all of his artistic ability and talent. His *musical* genius was not curtailed. He wrote for a church which believed that its principal task on earth was to adore the Creator of the Universe. Furthermore, this composer understood both the meaning of the text with which he worked and the reason *why* it had been selected as a part of the liturgical order of worship.

Now this is not always the case with the average non-liturgical church. Here, the philosophy of worship may be just as sincere, as devout, and as logically constructed as that which governs practice in any liturgical denomination. But the musician who labors in this field often feels that there is no real unity which binds together the several items in the order of service. If he is a sincere and dedicated person, he does much pondering about the nature of worship—what it is and what it should do to and for those who participate in its exercise.

Just what is this thing that we call "public worship"? It is difficult to find a definition upon which all of us might agree—but thinking of the original root of the word, that is, "wor*th*-ship," does this not call for the *appreciation*, the *thankfulness to* and subsequently the adoration of and praise for a Divine Being? But, as an order of service is planned in which worship should take place, is such an ideal always reached and maintained? And, if not I fear that some of the time the fault lies with the choirmaster and clergyman who either hold to opposing points of view concerning the nature of worship or who just don't care.

In the early days of the church everything that was sung and said was designed to lead up to a great climactic act. The celebration of this sacrament no longer takes place each Sunday in our churches. So, what is music supposed to do with and for worship? What direction must it take?

There are those who propose that our services become sermon-centered. Here, the theme of the sermon regulates the choice of prelude, scripture, prayers, psalter readings, congregational hymns, the music during the offering—even the organ postlude. All of us can understand that there is great unity in such an order of worship. A man leaves his church carrying in his mind and heart the theme for the day. But, do you realize that such "thematic" services would need to be planned many months in advance? Think how extensive a choir library is needed under these circumstances and how skilled the choir must be with their music reading. What of the worshipper who is untouched personally by the theme or topic for a given Sunday? Because *everything* in the order of worship has been related to a given theme, he is not reached by any spiritual experience unless the topic just happens to "hit home" with him.

Another group decries this emphasis upon sermon and suggests instead that public worship take its unity and its inspiration from mood or feeling. Their argument goes this way: There are certain moods which are closely related to the worship experience—moods which grip and possess the one who truly communes with his God. These emotions are mystery, awe, adoration, penitence, praise, and contrition. We engage in public worship first by *being aware* of where we are; then with this knowledge at hand we wish *to adore*. This, in turn, is succeeded by the feeling of *contrition*—we are truly sorry for sins

However, suppose that our idea as ministers and as musicians is to serve up a brand of music that soothes and comforts and entertains our congregations. Then we choose a kind of music that is showy and saccharine and sentimental. We glorify the personal. We drag into the sanctuary music that belongs elsewhere.

19

and shortcomings. With the promise of grace and forgiveness, we *praise* and we consecrate ourselves to live better lives.

If music inspires *mood* and if these certain moods are a part of worship, why not select a particular kind of music that will inspire a specific emotion in the listener? This is the way that these friends would have music used in a service of worship. Something like turning the water on and off at the kitchen sink!

While there is something to be said for this concept of that which happens to the individual as he worships, can we honestly believe that all of us experience the same emotion at the same time? And any number of psychological experiments have proven that everyone does not respond in exactly the same way at the same time to a piece of music played or sung.

If we reject the sermon or theme centered service—if we cannot accept the idea of *mood* as being central to a proper service of worship—most of us will settle for a so-called "free" service in which only *some* of the several items in the order of worship are related to each other. Here is where the choirmaster and the minister have their troubles. Do you, with Anderson Scott, consider that "the accepted vehicle of worship is *sacrifice*"? Do you believe that true worship consists in looking *away* from ourselves and adoring the Almighty? Should we say with the prophet, "Holy, holy, holy is the Lord of hosts—the whole earth is full of *His* glory"? If we believe this, then everything in the service which we offer to God will be of the very best—including the music.

However, suppose that our idea as ministers and as musicians is to serve up a brand of music that soothes and comforts and entertains our congregations. Then we choose a kind of music that is showy and saccharine and sentimental. We glorify the personal. We drag into the sanctuary music that belongs elsewhere. We love to listen to the high notes of the soprano and the low tones of the bass soloists.

Henry Sloane Coffin, a distinguished leader of the Presbyterian Church, and a past president of Union Theological Seminary, says bluntly that "choir music in many congregations is a serious menace to common worship. It is not praise offered to God in the name of his devout people, but musical numbers rendered for their gratification, and ill calculated to assist or to voice their reverence toward God." Dr. Coffin speaks particularly of a selection which he calls "an atrocity titled 'My God and I' in which the singers assert that God and they talk and laugh and jest together as good friends ought to do." Says Dr. Coffin, "Such an irreverent ditty conjures up the scene of two cronies swapping stories on cracker barrels at a corner store." What would a poet of ancient Israel have thought of such presumptious familiarity with the high and holy God? Do we forget that "God is a Spirit, infinite, eternal, and unchangeable in his being, wisdom, power, holiness, justice, goodness, and truth?"

I can hear some of you saying, "Do you advocate, then, the use by the church of 'old' music—that sort of composition which is dull and dry to modern ears?" I reply in the words of Richard Gore of Oberlin College, who says, "What do we have in our religious life that does not stem from the past? The architecture most used in western churches, the Gothic, comes from the 12th century; many of our favorite hymns are translations of Latin poems of the first ten centuries of our era; the bulk of our scriptures, the old Testament, is well over 3000 years old. Just as the dramas of Shakespeare have outlived the productions of hundreds of dramatists since his time, so the great works of Lassus, Byrd, Schütz, and Bach will outlive the shallow, ersatz church music of a later day."

At this point I would again suggest that those who are concerned about the music program in any particular church need to be of one mind with regards to its purpose. This calls for frequent conference and discussion staff meetings, if you please. May I go a bit further and list for you some of the topics which might serve as a basis for earnest thought and exchange of ideas?

Let us put it in the form of a dialogue:

The *choirmaster* says to his *minister*:

What are your ideas—your definition of public worship? What are my responsibilities in this area? Where do my responsibilities for the music begin and end? What do *you* choose? What do *I* choose?

The hymns. You choose them but may I help you with the choice?

Should the congregation be encouraged to give their ideas on my selection of the anthems?

Should the minister select the choir?

The *minister* says to his *director of music*:

Why are the anthems so long?

Why must we have a musical response every five minutes or so in the service?

Why do you sing such difficult selections?

At times, your music serves to drain the congregation emotionally so that they cannot receive anything from the sermon. As one man has said: "Think of the music in church as an *avenue*. You are to pass *through* it. You are not to *dwell* in it."

The choirmaster speaks again:

Why not a music committee which is also a committee on *worship*? Let us have something more than an employment agency. Should not the members of this committee know something about music? Can

I would again suggest that those who are concerned about the music program in any particular church need to be of one mind with regards to its purpose. This calls for frequent conference and discussion: staff meetings, if you please.

21

they not interpret to the congregation the purposes of the music program? And if they *know* and understand what they are doing, should not all of the four C's (including the clergymen) listen to what they have to say?

Furthermore, says the director, does the congregation understand that, even though the children and youth choirs may not *sound* as effectively as do the adult singers, they are learning the principles of worship—how to be *reverent*, how to *praise*, how to *pray* through their participation in a worship service?

Now, it is the turn again of the *minister* as he speaks to the *music director*:

What are you doing with yourself so that you are recognized as a spiritual leader of your people? Are you interested in your choir only as *musicians* or as human beings and as fellow Christians? Are you devoted to the results we may obtain through all of the worship experience—or are you concerned only with the musical portions of the service?

Hopefully all will agree to this statement: Come, let us reason together! Can we not work as a team to find those elements in music which will make for its proper use in the worship service? Can we learn to use that music which possesses true dignity? Can we learn how to choose a fine text—a text which avoids superlatives, stays away from cliches, is not repetitious, and does not use constantly the personal pronoun? What of its musical setting? Can we avoid waltzes and marches? Do we understand that dotted rhythms suggest the dance? Are we aware that sudden changes in dynamics call attention to the music and not to the message which it conveys? Do we know that a melody constantly repeated carries the same effect? Can we avoid using a piece that is full of sweet and trite harmonies?

If we are willing to learn—to understand—to cooperate, the minister will know his hymnal from the *musical* as well as the textual standpoint. He will not always choose hymns just because he happens to like them. He will trust his minister of music and his worship committee. And, the minister of music will be the intelligent artist, yes, but also will become a true colleague in working to secure the proper results from *all* of worship and not just his own part in it.

Surely, all of us can agree with Henry Sloane Coffin when he writes that "Christians offering their worship are in the vastest fellowship imaginable." They hear:

The universal choir.
The sons of light exalt their Sire
With universal song.

Success seems most often to crown the efforts of a conductor who assumes the dual responsibility of performer and teacher. . . . As a basic requirement for success in our profession, performance is not enough. Whether choral music is sung by groups representing school, church, or community, the conductor must teach.—"The Nashville Symposium: 'A Cause for Celebration,'–" *The Choral Journal*, 1983.

22

Earth's lowliest and loudest notes
Her million times ten million throats
Exalt Him loud and long,
And lips and lungs and tongues of grace
From every part and every place
Within the shining of his face
The universal throng.

Can we not work as a team to find those elements in music which will make for its proper use in the worship service? Can we learn to use that music which possesses true dignity?

A New Program for Church Music

A lecture delivered to the national convention of the American Guild of Organists in Pasadena, California, July 1962.

Because I knew that I would be speaking in a church sanctuary and some might be present who would feel more at home with a text, I offer not one, but two. So that everything will be in order, one reading is selected from the Old Testament, the other from the New. Both are very familiar:

–1–

In the year that King Uzziah died, I saw the Lord sitting upon a Throne, high and lifted up; and his train filled the temple. Above him stood the seraphim: each had 6 wings: with two he covered his face, and with 2 he covered his feet, and with 2 he flew. And one called to another and said: "Holy, holy, holy is the Lord of hosts; the whole earth is full of his glory." And the foundations of the threshholds shook at the voice of him who called—and the house was filled with smoke. And I said: "Woe is me—For I am lost; For I am a man of unclean lips, and I dwell in the midst of a people of unclean lips; For mine eyes have seen the King, the Lord of Hosts!

Then flew one of the seraphim to me having in his hand a burning coal which he had taken with tongs from the altar. And he touched my mouth and said: "Behold this has touched your lips; your guilt is taken away and your sin forgiven." And I heard the voice of the Lord saying "Whom shall I send and who will go for us?" Then I said—Here I am! Send me. [Isaiah 6:1-8]

–2–

Ye are the salt of the earth—but if the salt hath lost its savor wherewith shall it be salted? It is henceforth good for nothing but to be cast out and trodden under foot by men. [Matthew 5:13]

While objectivity in such matters never is fully realized, there takes place from time to time in most fields of endeavor an evaluation of progress and a restatement of goal and purpose. This kind of analysis and summation is properly applied to all areas of learning and activity: the professional, the scientific, and the artistic. Interestingly enough, the first and the only attempt to chart the comtemporary position of church music in America began about 30 years ago with the work of Dr. Archibald Davison and Canon Winfred Douglas and has continued down to the present in the writings and lectures of Paul Hume, Luther Reed, Joseph Clokey, Paul Henry Lang, Charles Etherington, Erik Routley, and several others. These men have concerned themselves with the music of all Christian faiths and denominations. There is a common strain of urgency and admonishment, and some pessimism which runs through all of their pronouncements. Yet, and somewhat curiously, there seems to be some hesitancy to predict the future for church music, particularly if the "musical architect" is asked for a drawing with considerable detail in it.

It is the most obvious of statements that what we *are* bears a strong relationship to what we *have been*. This is the *raison d'etre* for the historian. And, any historian does not stop with a casual consideration of cause and effect in making his evaluation of the present and prognosis for the future. He considers the element of *time*: What *time* has done to force a result in the past and what it may do for a development yet to come.

May I hasten to say that in the next few minutes I do not propose to trace the history of church music. However, I am somewhat concerned that those who have been troubled (and properly so) with the present state of affairs in our profession too often have not considered this important factor of time and its effect for good or ill upon worship music. It took more than 600 years to bring chant to its highest point of fulfillment. Ten centuries more were required to perfect the forms of sacred polyphony. And then, I would remind you that figuratively speaking "the roof fell in" upon church music—particularly in its vocal manifestations. The influence of the operatic—the secular and the instrumental—the theological reforms from both within and without the church—the nationalistic upheavals which were political, economic, sociological—all of these forces dealt the music of the church a kind of blow from which it has never completely recovered. It took sixteen hundred years and more to build; only three and one-half centuries have passed since the Renaissance. Are we expecting too much, too soon?

Whether we like it or not, church music, like the worship practices which it is supposed to assist and to dignify, is going to reflect the social behavior and beliefs of the time and the place where it op-

The very essence of our art—what we are about—why music and people are so important—[is] namely: for the creation and recreation of that which is <u>beautiful</u>. Beauty in form—beauty in sound—and, hopefully, beauty in the wonderful transformation of the human spirit.—"Symposium Summary, Observations and Reflections," *Southwestern Musician*, December 1977.

erates. For example, the frontier has been the basic force which has shaped America's culture over the past 100 years. As Robert Stevenson points out in his monograph, variety and contrast are key words in describing the church music from 1860 to 1960. In 1860, congregations were still debating the merits of living-out the hymns, and church clerks to whom this responsibility formerly had been given were becoming teachers of singing schools during the week and choir directors on Sunday. While one usually heard the reed organ and the melodeon in a worship service, he could find other churches where congregational singing was supported by bass viol and clarinet as it had been done for many previous decades. Lowell Mason, William Bradbury, and Thomas Hastings were three composers and compilers whose hymns reached into almost every part of the country, but a large segment of the south and west worshipped comfortably and loudly with the white spiritual and the shape-note tradition.

Whether the purpose of a hymn was to "get up the spirit" or to bring about "a quick decision," the music was used in such a way that the singer could be directed towards any goal which the church might specify. At periodic intervals during the past century, various segments of the church were interested in foreign missions, the temperance problem, and in social action. At the appropriate time, hymns were composed and sung which reflected these areas of concern. The most successful revivalists and their song leaders, Dwight Moody and Ira D. Sankey; Billy Sunday and Homer Rodeheaver; Billy Graham and Cliff Barrow; called for decisions from the throng who listened each night, and the gospel and revival hymn—subjective, sweet, saccharine, and eventually studded with sixths—was their principal weapon in the fight against the Devil and his minions.

As rapidly as a metropolitan area could rise above the crudities of the frontier, its cultural pattern changed as business and industry became the dominating forces in the community. Church music, together with music of all kinds, possessed one basic requirement. It had to be fashionable. Since the source of musical style and fashion was to be found in Europe, church music looked to the metropolitan centers of the continent for guidance. So, from 1850 to 1925 (a length of time almost exactly approximating the madrigal period of three hundred years before), the stylish city church employed a quartet choir of operatic soloists who sang Dudley Buck and Harry Rowe Shelley together with Rossini and Gounod, and operated from a loft located directly to the front of the expectant congregation. Conveniently curtained, the soloists might screen themselves off at will and often did so during the minister's sermon.

This is the period of the Roosevelt and the Hook and Hastings organs, and perhaps the best of all in quality, those built by the John-

Whether we like it or not, church music, like the worship practices which it is supposed to assist and to dignify, is going to reflect the social behavior and beliefs of the time and the place where it operates.

27

sons—father and son. Unfortunately, the American passion for bigness infected the organ builders, and the small classic organs gradually developed into large instruments, orchestral in sound and complete with detached console, if desired. Builders were influenced to some extent by the craze for theatre organs, although the barnyard and jazz stops were not incorporated into the ecclesiastical instruments.

In the twenties, musical matters began to change slowly for the better. Why was this? Was it because of the enforced removal from an isolationism engendered by the first World War? Did the great *Motu proprio* on church music of Pope Pius X issued in 1903 begin to have an effect in Roman circles, particularly when it was substantiated so emphatically by Pius XI in 1928? Was it because of the increased importance attached to the education of the clergy and the growth in numbers and importance of theological seminaries? Perhaps one would rightly expect that the influence of the American Guild of Organists and other professional organizations was beginning to have an effect upon the quality of church music. Why was it that liturgical practices now began to draw the interest of many who formerly had been unmoved by such forms of worship? Perhaps those who served church music began to see the work and hear the admonitions of a comparatively small number of earnest disciples who pled for a return to basic principles of worship and for a standard of good taste and beauty in the music to be selected for church usage. You know these men: Archibald Davison and Lynnwood Farnham, Horatio Parker, and Peter Lutkin, Canon Winfred Douglas, and Clarence Dickinson; John Finley Williamson, F. Melius Christiansen, John Smallman, Father William J. Finn, and Luther D. Reed. And to these names I think that the organ world would add those of Walter Holtkamp, Ernest Skinner, and G. Donald Harrison.

Rather suddenly, it seemed, there became available for use an exciting and a new kind of repertoire. No longer did organists have to play Guilmant and Wolstenholme on every recital program. Choirmasters found available for use new or republished editions of Bach and Schütz, the sixteenth century masters, composers in the idiom of the Russian Church, and the great English School of Church Music— and many others. To sing this material, conductors formed a cappella choirs almost before they knew how to spell the word. Universities and colleges planned curricula related to liturgics and church music; eager neophytes attended master classes which were planned to instruct in the proper technique of service playing or the specialized training of choristers. Vested choirs became commonplace. Furthermore, many churches were not satisfied with the sponsorship of one choral unit. They expanded their choral forces until choirs of all ages took their turns in singing for the several services of worship.

The thirties witnessed a continued and expansive flurry of activity related to church music. Summer camps, institutes, additions to repetoire, new techniques, and a dazzling kind of literature to explain their use poured from the presses. Organizations were formed of individuals interested in choral conducting, in hymns, in the development of children's choirs. Perhaps, however, the period of the 1930's was most notable for two great innovations which had a special and lasting relationship to church music. These were the radical changes in organ design—the beginning of the return to the classic organ, and the new editions of church hymnals which were sponsored by almost every major denomination and edited by outstanding church musicians.

In 1933, a book by Archibald T. Davison, *Protestant Church Music In America*, startled and sometimes infuriated church musicians and caused the thinking members of the profession to look closely at their philosophy and practice as implied in music and worship. Humorous and critical, earnest and thoughtful, ironic without being cynical, Dr. Davison attempted to set down in logical fashion his concept of an ideal musical practice and the materials which would be used in carrying forward such a service. He put aside the idea that general characteristics or moods were intrinsic in any music, that there exist any ethical powers in music, and that music seldom was rendered in such an ideal manner that it made its hearers properly receptive to religious teaching. Rather, said Davison, the noblest use of church music is as a sacrifice—an oblation which we offer in the name of the Almighty. There should be nothing of the subjective, of the egocentric in its selection, its performance, and its effect upon those who participate as worshippers. Because the sacrifice is to consist of that music which is in its suggestion apart from the world of everyday thoughts and experiences, Dr. Davison lists as materials these musical classifications: plainsong, 16th century polyphony, the Reformation chorale, the anthems of the Reformation and 17th century Protestant composers, 17th century English composers, certain pieces of 18th century geniuses, some 19th century music (mostly Mendelssohn), and occasional works of inspired composers (namely Bach and Handel), modern Russian music, and a few anthems of Gustav Holst, Ralph Vaughan-Williams, and Healey Willan.

I think it safe to say that this, in outline form, would be a new program for church music proposed by Dr. Davison. While I admire his scholarship, his devotion to high ideals, and the tremendous performance goals which were his constant achievement, I would raise these questions concerning his proposals. First, in the midst of his righteous indignation, did Dr. Davison consider how far American church music had moved in philosophy and practice in less than a century's time? Second, will the worshipper make use of that which he cannot understand or appreciate? Third, is there to be nothing of a subjective nature in worship? Is it wrong for the worshipper to expect a renewal of faith, the giving of comfort—the assurance of pardon?

Rather suddenly it seemed, there became available for use an exciting and a new kind of repertoire. No longer did organists have to play Guilmant and Wolstenholme on every recital program. Choirmasters found available for use new or republished editions of Bach and Schütz, the sixteenth century masters, composers in the idiom of the Russian Church, and the great English School of Church Music—and many others.

But, there are others who have formulated their new programs for church music. Let Paul Hume speak for the Roman Catholic musicians from the pages of his published volume entitled, *Catholic Music*. He says:

Some weeks before the encyclical was released (he refers to "The Discipline of Sacred Music" issued by Pope Pius XII in 1955), I made myself a list of the problems which seem to me to loom largest in the mind of the conscientious Church musician today. This choice was based on my own experience and on the views of the 468 people who generously lent me their thoughts and experiences for use in this book. Not all Church musicians, of course, face all of these problems all of the time, but it is a rare and happy man indeed who has not worried over one of them at one discouraged moment or another:

(1) The feeling that he is working without the full support or interest of the authorities who employ him.

(2) The feeling that the precepts of the *Motu proprio*, on which he would like to base his entire *modus operandi*, are not regarded by his pastor or bishop as actually binding upon him or them.

(3) The knowledge that in many places the labor of Popes, scholars and musicians in restoring the chant to its proper place in the liturgy is absolutely without fruit because of the prejudices of a few "key" men.

(4) The feeling that hymnody had sunk to a point beyond reclaim because no one with real authority had taken a stand on the dignity and artistic integrity necessary to hymns.

(5) The knowledge that no matter how hard the individual parish or diocese worked at its music, no widespread improvement could come about without a definitive program of education for the clergy of the future.

Reading the encyclical for the first time, therefore, was in the nature of a revelation, for all five of these vexing items are up for the most penetrating discussion.

Towards the end of his letter, "The Discipline of Sacred Music," Pope Pius XII says to the bishops of the world: "It is our hope that whoever in the Church supervises and directs the work of sacred music under your leadership may be influenced by our encyclical letter to carry on this glorious apostolate with new ardor and effort, generously, enthusiastically, and strenuously."

There can be little doubt that Church musicians all over the world will be influenced by the encyclical. The mere fact that the Holy Father saw fit to issue such a document—the only encyclical issued during the year of his illness—is an incredible gift to the morale of those who labor in this particular vineyard.

By reaffirming the importance of music in the eyes of the Church and by bringing the Church's clear wishes in the matter to the immediate attention of the hierarchy, the Holy Father has indeed given us a reason for "new ardor and new effort."

For Paul Hume the *Motu proprio* contains all that is needed in the way of a church music program. There are those within the Roman Catholic Church, however, who would question that the old music would answer every liturgical need. Robert Stevenson quotes Father John Boyd, a Jesuit, as writing these words:

> Liturgical art is the human reaction to the Christian Revelation. Being human, it should have the time-placed element inherent in human nature. Admittedly Gregorian music has attained high perfection as a vehicle of Catholic worship. But to freeze church music in the Gregorian neume or church architecture in the Gothic arch would be fatal.

And then Father Boyd goes on to make this significant comment:

> Personally, I have still to find Gregorian melodies to express as aptly as vernacular hymns what the Western heart means in hailing Our Lady. . . and Gregorian anthems to equal the Christmas carols that have grown out of the soil of the simple peasant heart.

Perhaps the most respected musician in the Lutheran tradition is Luther D. Reed. He has been personally involved in the liturgical movement of the last 50 years, has been chairman of the Joint Commission which prepared *The Service Book and Hymnal* published four years ago by eight Lutheran bodies in America, is an honorary member of the American Guild of Organists and has been an officer of the Hymn Society. Here is his outline of a theory of music which he says "liturgical communions may hold aloft as a true ideal." This is his program for church music:

> (1) Music should enter the sanctuary to serve. Our theology must rule our liturgics; our liturgics must rule our music.
> (2) Church music must be music of the church. There must be a union of pure text and pure music.
> (3) Service music may have congregational emphasis with choral participation (the Lutheran service); or choral emphasis with congregational participation (the Anglican service). A concertistic character it must *not* have.
> (4) Service music may be melodic but should not be strongly rhythmic. It is strongly modal and largely vocal. Dr. Reed quotes Richard Wagner as saying "If church music is ever to be restored to its original purity, vocal music must oust the instrumental and occupy the place this has usurped."
> (5) Music in the service of the church should satisfy the canons of *beauty* as well as of liturgical propriety and churchly purity.
> (6) We should select a balanced musical program from both ancient and *modern* sources.

In September, 1960, Robert Shaw, Director of the Chorale which bears his name and Associate Conductor of the Cleveland Orchestra, was installed as Minister of Music of the First Unitarian Church in Cleveland. On that occasion he made certain remarks which could be rightfully considered as his credo concerning music and worship in a liberal church. I would like to read a part of his statement to you for I think that it will raise certain questions in our minds which might be summed up in this manner: How far can we go along with the author in his description of a church music program? To what extent do we disagree? In his own inimitable way let Mr. Shaw tell you some of the things which he would propose as a part of his program for church music:

> Knowing, then, at least some few things concerning the natures of music and worship and liberalism, what should be our purposes and our program, what shall be our forces and our forms of worship in the liberal church?
>
> We propose concerning our music that nothing but the best is good enough. One does not support value by subscribing to rubbish. For men of good will and good reason there is no nourishment in a sanctimonious swill flushing the sound-trough.
>
> This raises a fair question: on what grounds, and upon whose authority, are we to decide that which is worthy and that which is worthless in music for worship. That is a pertinent question, for may not one man's Bach be another's "Old Rugged Cross"?
>
> I would submit to you four criteria which may help us in our evaluations:
>
> The first is that of *motivation*. Let us say right out that purity of purpose dignifies. Moody and Sunday and Graham are not bad men. And 4,000 young people are not proved irredeemable by chanting "Softly and Tenderly Jesus is Calling" in Madison Square Garden.
>
> But these things are also true:
>
> They would have had a much richer experience had they been privileged to sing, from the end of the *St. Matthew Passion*, "Now has the Lord been laid to rest . . . My Jesus, sweet good-night."
>
> Moreover, they could not have remained long unconvinced as which of the pieces of music was truer witness to the qualities of Jesus of Nazareth.
>
> One could choose other examples in which, from the standpoint of motivation, there is *no* conceivable hiding-place: say, a Gregorian *Pater Noster* vs. that contemporary chalice of profitable piousity [sic], Malotte's *Lord's Prayer*.
>
> Motivation dignifies, but it is not enough.
>
> A second criterion must be *craftsmanship*. Music is a craft, and has its laws—and within comfortable limits these are knowable. There is decent, honestly constructed music, and there is stupid, miserably constructed music. We do not ask this moment that the building be an unassailable masterpiece of art, but that it have at least the mortar and brick and foundation specified in the contract.
>
> In the third instance great music will have an *historical perspective*, an aesthetic field, an originality which has origins. This criterion is close to what we mean by "style," and given a consonance of motivation and craftsmanship and style, we are a long way towards insuring the value of our repertoire.
>
> For finally, of course, there remains the hope that our work of art may be the product of the great artist, "evidenced not only by his capacity of ordering his experience but also by his capacity of having his experience."
>
> Only the best is good enough.
>
> The second of our purposes should be that nothing which has stirred the heart and mind of man to the consideration of creation of

The feeling of singing and expressing one's own inmost thoughts through the words and music of two great artists, the poet and the composer, is a great thrill. Then, when you do it with other people, you become part of a group, so that literally what you produce is greater than the sum total of all the individual efforts. It's rather a great thing.— "Objectives For a Choir," *The Choral Journal,* November 1971.

worth—in whatever time or place—can be foreign to worship in the liberal church.

This means that we are privileged to include in the matrix of the sacred, materials which in certain traditions have heretofore been considered secular. Not all of the prophets are dead, not all of the World is in one volume, not all of the testaments of beauty are sealed. Wherever the word has been made flesh—in Beethoven or Shakespeare, Scarlatti or Blake or Lincoln—it should be made welcome in this church.

This also judges in some detail the truth and breadth of our liberalism; for it demands that we perceive in a Palestrina mass, a Bach cantata on the resurrection, a Gregorian or Buddhist chant, a Negro Spiritual or a Mormon hymn man's hunger for God and his will for good.

Mr. Shaw then goes on to tell his listeners about the materials and personnel with which the music will be made. The organ is a Holtkamp, the piano is a Steinway, and there is a harpsichord and a string quartet. You will be happy to know that he speaks glowingly of the work of his organist. Then he concludes his remarks in this way:

The tradition of this church, shared by most of native American protestantism, is centered around its preaching. We have not sought to alter that, but to enrich, and implement and fulfill it. Our services have been formed and our music selected for some months ahead in consultation with our minister and with direct reference to the subjects and materials of his preaching.

We propose that music, our part in it and our response to it, shall be as worthy an act of worship as the spoken word, our occasional part in it and our response to it. You will note on our order of worship no prelude, no offertory and no postlude. Music for worship should be too essential and too significant to be used as diversion or cloak to cover the sounds of assembly and departure.

For finally it is our desire to create for a certain period each week out of worthy things an integrity of sound and sight and reason, which shall be its own reason for being and our reason for being here.

That this shall be a place where the whole man, in the company and affection of his fellow man, honestly may love the Lord his God with all his heart and all his soul and all his mind.

I began this talk with the reading of two scriptural texts. Perhaps you are wondering about the relationship of either of these to programs of church music. The implication in the passage from the Sermon on the Mount is rather clear—"If the salt have lost its savor wherewith shall it be salted? It is henceforth good for nothing but to be cast out. . . . "

The Davisons and the Reeds and the Shaws have each developed their programs for church music. What are your ideas and standards and goals? Do these busy days find you "salted" with imagination— with a zeal to develop a program which is aesthetically acceptable, helpful to every worship experience, and challenging to those who work with you? It seems to me that regardless of the denomination or its form of worship, a program of church music will succeed only if

Do these busy days find you "salted" with imagination— with a zeal to develop a program which is aesthetically acceptable, helpful to every worship experience, and challenging to those who work with you?

he who directs it possess a philosophy and the desire and the skill to implement it. A new program begins with the one at the center of things.

At this point I am not about to question you on your musicianship, the number of courses which you took in college, and the significance of the letters which you are entitled to place after your name. I *do* happen to believe that church musicians like most musicians do not listen to enough music. I would guess that those seated in front of me

Howard Swan conducting
at Occidental College, 1937

hear many organ recitals in the course of a year—but do you try to increase your understanding and appreciation for other forms of music? If you do not, then how can you stretch your imagination, how can you possess that intangible something that we call "good taste"?

If you call yourself a "good musician"—then you will find a way to use the best in contemporary compositions. Not only will your choir sing these selections and you will play them—but with an imaginative seeking out of the proper committees and head of church groups you will acquaint them with the significant days, occasions, ceremonies and so forth that should be dignified with a composition commissioned and composed especially for the event. When you and others like you find that contemporary music speaks eloquently in the service of the church, you will insist that the very best of our living composers write in this idiom. It *is* possible for the millennium to be closer than we think. Why not give it a shove?

There are *educational* as well as *musical* implications in the planning for a program of church music. This is the point at which we build an appreciation for the finest kind of music among our parishioners. And, friends, may our sacred concerts be developed from materials which are needed for our own particular situation; rather, let us not plan a program which will "look good in print" or will "show that fellow down the street that we, too, know what is going on."

The church musician who believes in education will *read*. He will enthusiastically support choir camps, workshops and institutes. Not only will he align himself with professional organizations, but he will insist that these groups sponsor educational activities related to church music, that they "spread the good word" by means of printed materials and that they (and he) will speak out forcefully and fearlessly on important and sometimes controversial subjects. Some topics might well be these: (1) Shall a soloist sing in a service of worship? (2) Business ethics and church music. (3) Salaries for church musicians. (4) Pensions for full-time church musicians.

It is in the area of the psychological—of social psychology—or just plain human relations, if you will, that so many church musicians seem to lack knowledge and understanding. Too often the organist or choirmaster is a master of technique; but in his desire to know more about the physical and the technical, he has built an ivory tower about himself and fails to recognize or respond to the human desires for *cooperation* and *sympathy* and *love*. Why—some church musicians don't even know how to express thanks to a colleague! Do we understand and accept the *honesty* of human beings, particularly boys and girls? Do we understand human differences, the recognition of group leaders, the "whenness" as Bob Shaw would put it of *appeal* and *command* and *reward*? Have we forgotten the difficulty that young people have in *making decisions*? Can we create experiences of beauty to evoke the

But the man or woman who is possessed of true spiritual conviction understands the meaning of the term "minister of music." They are willing to go the extra mile. They accept the responsibility for all of the music in their church including that sung and played in the church school. Because they are helped to grow in their spiritual life through the music which they have had a share in creating, they understand that all of their choristers may have the same experience.

35

desired response in a boy or girl? Do we understand that the child in our choir lives in two worlds—one a world of fantasy and imagination and the other the very *real present*—that which is happening right now? Do we take advantage of these and many other precious bits of knowledge to plan rehearsals and programs and other activities as we labor for our own particular church?

We find ourselves in a most unusual kind of professional situation. So much of that which we will accomplish in a church music program is conditioned by that which people are willing to do with and for us. Ours is a *volunteer* kind of operation. How effective are we at working with other volunteers? This is what I mean by the "psychological" training and understanding needed by one who proposes to build a proper program for church music.

Finally, there is a last and most important matter for the church musicians to consider. I speak of their own spiritual development. I am not pleading for the acceptance of any particular belief or creed or dogma. But the man or woman who is possessed of true spiritual conviction understands the meaning of the term "minister of music." They are willing to go the extra mile. They accept the responsibility for all of the music in their church including that sung and played *in the church school*. Because they are helped to grow in their spiritual life through the music which they have had a share in creating, they understand that all of their choristers may have the same experience. They believe that this is a very powerful argument for the maintenance of a system of multiple choirs. They accept every section of the "Declaration of Religious Principles of the American Guild of Organists," and particularly they adhere to these final paragraphs:

> We believe that at all times and at all places it is meet, right, and our bounded duty to work and to pray for the advancement of Christian worship in the holy gifts of strength and nobleness; to the end that the Church may be purged of her blemishes, that the minds of men may be instructed, that the honor of God's House may be guarded in our time, and in the times to come.
>
> Wherefore we do give ourselves with reverence and humility to these endeavors, offering up our works and our persons in the Name of Him, without Whom nothing is strong, nothing is holy. Amen.

For such a church musician, Isaiah's description of the worship of the Almighty is an ever present ideal and inspiration. It is he who will say: "And I heard the voice of the Lord saying, whom shall I send and who will go for us? (And he will answer) Here am I; send me. . . . "

I should like to close this statement with the words with which Robert Stevenson ended his report on 100 years of American church music, included in an anthology published by G. Schirmer. He says:

> So long as America continues diverse enough to be a land in which 256 different denominations can flourish we must continue to

expect diversity in church music. The tares will probably continue to grow up taller than the wheat; but at least some wheat does grow. The musically sensitive church goer who considers the tares will justify himself in some such words as Charles Ives's father used. Someone asked Ives's father (who was a professional musician) how he could "stand to hear of John Bell (who was the best stone mason in town) bellow off-key the way he does at camp meetings?" Ives's father replied: "Old John is a supreme musician. Look into his face and hear the music of the ages. Don't pay too much attention to the sounds. If you do, you may miss the music."

The "Lost" Art of Inspiration

An honorary life member of the Choral Conductors Guild in California, Swan gave this address at the Guild's convention in June 1968. It was published in the September/October issue of the CCG's Journal *that same year and later in* The Choral Journal.

I selected as the title of this talk with you (I hope not at you) "The 'Lost' Art of Inspiration" and the word "lost" has a quotation mark around it—at the beginning and at the end. Of course, when a word is put in quotation marks, the question is whether or not inspiration has been lost by those of us who have been inspired in the past.

Now, the dictionary defines the term "inspire" to mean, and I'm quoting, "to affect, so as to enliven, animate, impel or stimulate." And some synonyms which the same volume gives for inspiration are these: "enthusiasm, motivation, to prompt, evoke, GOAD, to get up the spirit, to encourage, to excite, to persuade, to wheedle, coax, or convince." I'm wondering if the time has not come, particularly this year, to ask ourselves, "Has inspiration become a lost art, a lost cause with church musicians?"

In October, 1968, the Choral Conductors' Guild in California will observe its 30th anniversary. Thirty years ago, we who were interested in founding this organization could hardly contain our enthusiasm for music and all we thought it could accomplish for the Church.

Now, just for a very few moments, I'd like to paint a picture of that time. During the 20's, for the most part, church musicians had very poor music to be used in the services of the Church—poor literature, Victorian anthems; the "trinity" in the Church—speaking musically, not theologically—were Dudley Buck, Charles Gounod, and Theodore Dubois. Or if you wanted to look in another direction, the great masterpieces which all of us hoped we would have the opportunity to direct *once* before we retired were: "The Messiah," "The Elijah," and "The Creation." We didn't go beyond this. In the smaller churches when, then, as now, Christmas was a great time—what did they sing? They sang a Christmas cantata; and it didn't make very much difference what the name of the cantata might be, for it was always the same. It always began with the prophecy sung by the full choir, or a whiskey tenor. And then the Angels' chorus will now sing the Coming of Christ: the women's chorus. The Shepherds: a trio. And then a change of pace, the Wisemen: the male chorus of course!

Do you realize that until the late 30's it was almost impossible to buy a piece of music by Heinrich Schütz in this country? Or by Dietrich Buxtehude or Bruckner?

39

always sung rather slowly so that the full rich mellifluous chords we call today "barbershop" could be heard by all in the church. Folks, some of you remember these Christmas cantatas. And then we always went on to the "pièce de résistance" for the soloist in the choir—the Madonna's Lullaby. Don't you remember? And finally the great triumphant chorus, the triumphant chorus into which was woven, rather cleverly we thought, all of the prominent Christmas carols—"Adeste Fidelis," "Silent Night." This was always the Christmas cantata. And this was the kind of literature with which we worked.

Then along came the 30's and all of a sudden things exploded. We had the opportunity to study with master teachers: John Smallman, Father Finn, F. Melius Christiansen, John Finley Williamson, Clarence Dickinson. As we became excited and as we developed organizations to perform these works, the publishers began to bring out some literature that was worthwhile. Then the next question: How do you practice? How do you rehearse? How do you prepare a group to sing this literature? This involved all of the development of choral and vocal techniques. Then we found there were differences of opinion, as far as the KIND OF TONE which should be used. Workshop after workshop and demonstration after demonstration were given on the subject of Choral Tone. It was very exciting, particularly when we, for the first time perhaps, began to sing pieces of music unaccompanied. Oh, we had to learn how to spell "a cappella," but it was so worthwhile.

We learned there were composers we had never heard of before. Do you realize that until the late 30's it was almost impossible to buy a piece of music by Heinrich Schütz in this country? Or by Dietrich Buxtehude or Bruckner? (He wrote those symphonies, didn't he?) And there was yet to come, of course, all of the conversation, all of the demonstrations, all of the work with style in music. This was to come later.

Were these the good old days? Am I simply evoking a time of nostalgia? May I remind you that in 1936 there was one of the bitterest wars that has ever been found on this globe, the Spanish Civil War? In 1937, the Chinese-Japanese War and the rape of Nanking? In 1938, the same year in which the Choral Conductor's Guild was born, this was the year of Munich. This was the year of the Anschluss. And we all knew that war was coming. Of course, it finally came the following summer. I somehow sense that many of us present here in 1968, involved in church music, are baffled, are discouraged, and if we face it properly, are somewhat frightened. We see our churches confused, apathetic, and sometimes divided over social issues. We find it is impossible to please people as we once did. Do people respond to your ideas as they once did? If what I hear is true, they don't! And if what I hear is true, and this is what gives me great concern, a lot of people in our

An optimistic realist is. . . . calm and industrious, patient and imaginative, and properly curious about individuals. He has a sense of humor. He's moved by beauty in all its manifestations.— **"Humanistic Education," Little Rock, 1979.**

40

profession, perhaps some of you listening to my voice, are almost getting to the place that you say, "What's the use! What do I do now—where do I *go* now?" Standards for the programs and the objectives with which we have always been successful no longer seem to motivate people. People often just don't care about our music, and the newer forms of music-making baffle us—the folk masses, and the guitars, and the texts which speak of revolt and which seem to have very little literary merit are strange. They're strange because we seem to have no way in which we can test their effectiveness for worship.

Then we look about us. Perhaps never before has this world been the scene of so much malice, misunderstanding and hatred, man against man, generation against generation, group against group, country against country, suspicion, anger, violence, fear, mistrust seen and heard, discussed and written about in all hours of the day and night. Objectives, goals, standards—these seem now almost to be decadent terms which have been replaced by vitriolic criticism or just plain apathy. Many men seem to prefer a mere existence to the excitement of really living a life. There is something alarming nowadays in the fact that too many followers are thinking the thoughts voiced by leaders who *obviously* have no answers. *Faith, Hope, Love!* Does it not become more difficult to see these truths functioning in today's world?

Now I submit to you, ladies and gentlemen, that it takes a *very great* person, a *Very Great Person* (and notice that I don't say a very great musician) it takes a *very great person* to be an inspiring choral conductor in these times, because the choral conductor has to be, he has to continue to be, the leader of his group. When they are confused, and confused on almost any issue, *he must know.* When they are frustrated, he must be composed and assured. He must have answers for himself which run the entire gamut, not only of his technical training, but of his personal equipment, his musicianship, his mind, his speech, his industry, his sensitivity to sound, his ability to communicate with his choristers. All of this has to be of a higher caliber than ever.

If inspiration *is* a lost art among conductors, such has happened because we have decided to give up, to "throw in the towel," to admit that we are too tired, or too old, or too confused to seek out new sources for a rekindling of an enthusiasm for our work. And, as is always the case, do we blame ourselves for this? No, we're human, aren't we—all of us? We blame circumstances, we blame events, we blame other people that we can't do it any more because of the minister, or the music committee, or the people in this church, or the vacation spot where the people go, or because the young people in my church don't understand me.

It seems to me that, as has always been the case since the year One, we have to face the situation by *facing ourselves.* It hasn't changed. We have to continue to have faith in ourselves and our pro-

It takes a very great person, a Very Great Person (and notice that I don't say a very great musician) it takes a very great person to be an inspiring choral conductor in these times, because the choral conductor has to be, he has to continue to be the leader of his group. When they are confused, and confused on almost any issue, he must know. When they are frustrated, he must be composed and assured. He must have answers for himself which run the entire gamut, not only of his technical training, but of his personal equipment, his musicianship, his mind, his speech, his industry, his sensitivity to sound, his ability to communicate with his choisters. All of this has to be of a higher caliber than ever.

grams. And if this is true, we are going to look to *ourselves* for our own improvements.

How long since you've thought over some of these things that I'm going to name now? (And I'm asking myself the question and— you've heard me say this before—this applies to me as well as to you.) I'd like to ask every choral conductor here: How well do you hear? How well do you listen? How much do you hear at a rehearsal? When you listen to a performance, whether live or recorded, *how* do you listen to it? Oh, anyone can sit back and listen aesthetically. And anyone can sit back and listen critically. This is not what I am talking about. Do you listen *technically*? If not, why don't you practice it? If you are a singer, where do you get if you never vocalize and you never practice with your own voice? If you propose to be a listener, where are you ever going to get if you don't practice listening?

I suggest to you that listening has to be done on three levels. The first one is the easiest one. WHAT is happening? Oh, we're pretty expert with this, most of us. We can say, can't we, that is too fast, that is too slow, that is too loud, that is too soft, they're not doing this right thing with that phrase, it is a little out of tune on this particular chord. That's the WHAT in my book. In my definition of listening, that's the WHAT. That is fairly simple.

But now let us step up to another level. WHY is it happening? Not the WHAT anymore, but WHY did that conductor do that? Can you guess? Was it because this particular conductor had an interest in a certain style or a certain tone, or in a certain kind of interpretation? Is that the reason why that performance to which you are listening sounds like that? That is what I mean by the WHY.

What is the hardest level of all? HOW. HOW. Isn't it logical that if you hear something that you don't like, that you can figure out *why* you don't like it? Don't you want to be smart enough so you'll never be caught doing that same thing? And if you listen to a performance and you *do* like it, and you figure out why it is that you like it, wouldn't you like to be able to do the same thing? That's what I mean by the HOW. Yes, this is difficult to do, but with practice you can do it. And my friends, look what happens when you learn this and you march into a rehearsal and you are equipped with this kind of knowledge, motivation and inspiration—ah, it too will be there. In this day and age our people still *respect those who know what they're doing*. And in knowing what they are doing, *they don't waste time doing it*. And that's a part of the HOW too. Isn't it? How are you going to do it?

You can see how it is in so many rehearsals (and it's been this way for a long time, not just now.) Picture, I won't say an average choir, but picture a choir rehearsal. The choir sings through two pages. The director listens. She/he doesn't quite know what to do. So what does he say? "Now choir, don't you see what those words mean?" (But of course they see what they mean. They are in English!) But the director hasn't heard anything musical to correct so he *expounds* on the meaning of the written language—the spoken language, because he doesn't dare do anything with the musical language. And as he expounds, he gets caught up with the sound of his own voice. It sounds pretty good, so he makes quite a speech. After a little time, three or four sopranos begin talking; the one tenor talks to the two basses while the director is working with the altos. And then, after a time, he gets started again. Then again, stop, another lecture; sing, another lecture; sing, another lecture. And unfortunately, it works in inverse ratio. The lecturing gets longer and longer and longer, and the singing gets shorter and shorter and shorter. Now what I'm trying to say is this: if we really know the HOW, are there not some kinds of things we do at the rehearsal *by drill?* Are there not some kinds of things that are done at rehearsal without ever talking about them because you figured out ahead of time that you are such a good communicator as you conduct that there is no use to talk about those things? So why waste time talking about them? And there are some kinds of things that you want the people in your choir to illustrate to each other. Isn't that right? You don't want to make a lecture about it. And maybe there are some things, if you play very well, that you'll want to show them *How* by playing at the piano or the organ. And maybe, if you sing well, there are some of the things that you're going to do that you'll illustrate with your own voice. Now, if all of these and various many other kinds of HOW's take place at your rehearsal, isn't your rehearsal going to be interesting instead of "talk-sing, talk-sing, talk-sing, talk-sing." It seems to me so. So all of this, it seems to me, comes from the first idea that I speak of. How well do you listen? And if you don't listen very well, why don't you do something about it?

Second (and many of you have heard me say this before, and this is a never ending quest)—how *tasteful* are you these days? How do you respond to beauty? Do you really have an inherent good taste for everything? Now again, doesn't this have to be practiced? Our artist friends tell us so. Our writers tell us so. Certainly we find this true, don't we, in working with people? Is there not beauty in people? Don't you have to work at it to find it, sometimes very hard?

And the little ones are persons too, aren't they? Not just because they are cute, but they are persons. And nowadays how about those young people? Are they persons? *You bet they are!* Do they speak a strange language? It should not be strange to you and to me, my friends, if we take the trouble to find out what they are talking and thinking about. I won't embarrass you in this particular way, but I wonder how many of you listen to at least one "Rock" program per week? Now, if you don't, how are you going to know what their terminology is, their heroes, the way they think? And you expect to com-

In this day and age our people still respect those who know what they're doing. And in knowing what they are doing, they don't waste time doing it.

43

municate with them? They don't *know* enough to come up with *our* language, even if they dared. They will think a great deal of you and me if we talk *their* language. This doesn't mean, of course, that we have to *believe,* that we have to *admire*; but to establish some kind of communication, we have to begin to *think* as they do. This is what I mean by recognizing *beauty*, of understanding *human beings*. It's the first step.

Thirdly, what about this business of choice of repertoire? Oh, I'm not talking about whether you pick repertoire because you say it's a good piece of music or not. No, at this particular point, I'm far more interested in whether you know what you conduct best. Now, you are going to tell me that you conduct every piece of music equally well? You probably have two or three kinds of music with which you feel comfortable, which you conduct and you know that you conduct this the best. For goodness sakes, without slackening in your attempts to do everything equally well, find out what kind of music you do best and learn everything you can about it so that it becomes much more meaningful, so that you *burst* with your enthusiasm as far as the choir is concerned. Motivation? Yes, I think so.

In the next place it seems to me that if you're really interested in this business of inspiring people, a lot of us will have to know much more than we do at the present time, about the *voice*, about singing. For the life of me, I cannot understand some of our people in the choral field who presume to work with individuals who have vocal instruments and who know nothing at all about the vocal instrument. We would *never* accept this from our great symphonic conductors. Imagine a person standing on a podium not knowing what is capable of coming from a violin or a clarinet or a flute! And yet we stand up in front of our people and assume that the high voice is the same as the low voice—and that every vowel sound is the same and that the men are just like the women—and all personalities are alike. Amen!—and all we have to do is start 'em and stop 'em. Wouldn't it be wonderful if some of us, some of you sitting in front of me, in the year 1968-69 would say, "In every way possible, I'm going to find out more about *singing because I direct singing!*" Why if you will do this, my friends, when you haven't known very much before, do you know what is going to happen to you? Your conducting is going to change, you're going to change as a personality, your posture is going to change, I think I can almost say with certainty that you will look and feel ten years younger. (That's a kind of incentive right there, isn't it?)

As another objective for this next year, I would hope that we could learn a great deal more about communication. As some of you will remember, I talked about this at the Convention last year. It seems to me that, no matter whether we read it, or we see it, or listen to it on television, and no matter whether it's a part of a profession or business, or the arts, politics, or governments, everybody is talking about *communications*. Isn't this the reason why countries don't get along? Isn't this the reason why generations don't get along with each other?

Now, in working out this business of communication, I am suggesting that, without going into it in detail, we can afford to sit down and say to ourselves, "What do I do to communicate? How do I appear to the people with whom I have been in contact each week?"

How do you appear to your choir? Have you ever thought of that? How do you stand? Do you say the same old cliches from week to week? Did you ever stop to think, for instance, how many times we say to the choir, "Now attack! Now sing!" Can't we find different ways to say that? We say it every week. I suppose what?—twenty-five times at a rehearsal, at least. Do you think that is going to register? What is the pitch of your speaking voice? How fast do you talk? Do you speak with a kind of mood that you are trying to engender in your choir? All of this is a part of communication. Or are you the kind of person that says, "NOW CHOIR, SING QUIETLY!"

How about the picturesqueness of your speech? Yet I've had so many people say, "Now you are going too far, Mr. Swan, that's going just too far! There are only certain people who are poets with words."

It would seem to me that it would be very wise in the matter of speech to look at the tempo of our speech, the pitch of our speech, and as I say, the picturesqueness that we use in our rehearsals. If you are not a poet with words, then why not figure out before the rehearsal begins, some extremely beautiful things to say about this phrase, or this place where you *know* those altos are going to flat, and write them down on a piece of paper? And then at the proper point in the rehearsal (you have them, of course, on your podium right along side of your music) and at that particular point, *make* the point with a perfectly beautifully-turned phrase or two. This can be done ahead of time. And when you work with this kind of self-study, don't you see how it increases your effectiveness with the choir?

But I can see where some of you will say, "I've done all of these things and it doesn't do any good. I'm still not very inspiring, even to myself, I'd like something new. I've got to set myself on fire *again*." Well, may I suggest to you that this is one thing that will do it.

I know some of you know this book, but I rather imagine because it is so new a great many of you do not. This is the book by Wilhelm Ehmann on *Choral Directing* (Augsburg). I submit that this book is going to be our "bible" for the next fifteen years in this country because we can't possibly catch up with this man. This doesn't mean that we're going to agree with everything that he says, not at all. But what do you do with a book, for example, that has chapters, and big ones, on "Body Movement in Choral Singing?" Have you seen this demonstrated in any clinics in this country lately? What do you do

How do you appear to your choir. Have you ever thought of that? How do you stand? Do you say the same old cliches from week to week? Did you ever stop to think, for instance how many times we say to the choir "Now attack? Now sing?" Can't we find different ways to say that?

45

with a director who says one of the most important things that can happen to a choir is to catch the symbolism of its own existence as a choir; and as a result of this, rehearsals and performances if possible should always be carried on in a circle? And he gives good reasons for it. What do you do with a man who has a whole section devoted to the "Singing of Canons," not because canons, necessarily, as he says, are great pieces of music; but what happens to your choir as a result of singing them? And another great section on "Unison Singing?" Well, we have thought in terms of unison singing in this country as sort of being third and fourth grade stuff, haven't we? *This is a BOOK! This is really a "bible"!* This man directs the School of Church Music in Herford, Germany, head of the Cantato Records, has a magnificent choir that has sung only once in this country, but travels regularly over the rest of the world, including Asia. This man is a *thinker* and is way out ahead of us. And this doesn't mean that you will accept all of his ideas. *But will he make you THINK! This* is the thing you need for inspiration.

Secondly, if it's going to come, it's going to come and why don't you jump in it? What am I talking about? The music with the guitar accompaniment—and the vibraphones and the string bass. Are you going to be so intolerant that you will say that it doesn't belong without ever having experienced it? Why don't you make this a summer where you'll fill your ears with that sound? I suppose the most advanced school of choral writing at the present time where they are doing more with sacred music than any other place in the world is West Germany—where they really have their finest composers, secular composers if you please, writing sacred music. And what kind of accompaniment do you think it is? Vibraphone, guitar, drums, string bass. Don't you think it's time we better at least expose ourselves to it? I'm not arguing for it, but can you say it doesn't belong without knowing anything about it? Of course you can't.

I think in the last month I have had six different conductors say something like this to me: "You know, people just don't come to our musical services any more. They just won't come. They won't come and listen."

I say to them, "What time are you having them?"

"Oh, seven o'clock, eight o'clock, four-thirty."

I say to them, "How long have you had them that way?"

"Well, ever since I've been at the church that has been the hour for the musical service."

And I say, Why don't you try different hours? Try six o'clock at night followed by a supper. Try seven o'clock at night and precede it with a supper. Why don't you take every one of your musical services next year and put each one at a different time and find out *when* people will come—and if your audience changes or not? And it might be a very good thing for your church if you got your music committee and minister to agree that your choir members can stand out in front of the church (this seems to be the thing nowadays) as the people leave the church, and pass out petitions. What will be the petition? "As I am a member of this church, I agree to support the choirs in their musical services this year." And they sign their names. This is a *time* for experimentation. This is a time when we can't do it the same old way. We've got to be brave enough to try it a new way.

What are you doing with your choir ecumenically? How long since you have visited another choir in your community? I'm not talking about a Festival. Why don't you just go over and visit that *other* choir on their choir night and have them come over and visit with you? People *like* this kind of thing—or didn't you know it? Why do we always have to do it in the same old way?

What does your program of church music do to help people outside of the church? What is your choir program doing for the great social issues of today? Anything? Boy, we had better face this one! Are you a part of the great social evolution that is going on at the present time? You know, *sometime* when you are a great deal older than you are now, some little girl or some little boy is going to say to you, "What did *you* do in the Great Revolution in the 60's and 70's, grandmother, grandfather?" Because *this is* a revolution! What are we doing in it with our choirs? And since this is what our choirs are thinking about, if we are not doing anything—do you blame them for feeling uninspired?

Music finally comes alive through the agency of many personalities. Something wonderful happens which is not duplicated anywhere else on earth. You know what happens when you and your choir catch fire. They never forget it. They continue to talk about it. The spark which furnishes this inspiration comes from the conductor. He needs all the capabilities which I have been listing. But so many of these he must teach himself—much of the technical, the sensitivities, the appreciations, and most importantly, his response to the chorus before whom he stands. Now this takes hard work. It takes drive, and time, and strength, and sweat and some tears, and a fervent cultivation of joy and laughter. We never, even in these times, can afford to lose our sense of humor. It takes imagination and creativity. In my dictionary the outstanding conductor always is an optimistic realist. He is a realist in recognizing his own limitations but is not defeated by them. He is a realist when he evaluates constantly the ambitions of his choir. He shows his realism by his study, by planning his rehearsals, by experimentation (and this is the year for this), and by learning to know his people as individuals—not just as bodies, or names, or numbers. Yet he is an optimist, for his faith never wavers in himself, or his performers, and, most importantly for the music.

You know what happens when you and your choir catch fire. They never forget it. They continue to talk about it. The spark which furnishes this inspiration comes from the conductor. He needs all the capabilities which I have been listing. But so many of these he must teach himself—much of the technical, the sensitivities, the appreciations, and most importantly, his response to the chorus before whom he stands. Now this takes hard work. It takes drive, and time, and strength, and sweat and some tears, and a fervent cultivation of joy and laughter.

47

Don't you let what is going on around us these days "get you down"! WE HAVE MUSIC! Are all those things you have said to your choirs about music merely words? When you talk about the strength, and its emotional understanding and its giving of faith, have all those just been words? Are you going to let it down now? Are you not even going to try to search further for what we can do? We have *music*, an art which is wonderfully expressive in form and sound, in its content, and in its capacity to inspire. But what of ourselves? Surely these are

Faculty member,
Occidental College, 1955

the times which more than ever demand of us our study, our dedication, our patience, our good humor, and our faith. In this respect, times do not change. Today as always, the principal source for our inspiration must be *ourselves*.

Johann Sebastian Bach: Humanitarian, Musician, Theologian

At this unique service of the First United Methodist Church in Pasadena, California, on Sunday, April 1, 1979, Swan's sermon detailed Bach's life as husband, father, and teacher.

How many of us have had this experience? We have just finished reading a well-written novel or an absorbing biography. Perhaps we have seen a play or a motion picture where the characterizations as developed by the playwright or played by the actors are so powerful that they become for us actual flesh and blood personalities. Our imaginations have become so stimulated that in the days which follow we find ourselves becoming more and more attracted to these characters who have made such a deep impression upon us. At times their presence is so real that they seem to become our close friends. We wonder why they said this or that, and we speculate as to what has happened to their lives since we last saw or read of their adventures. We would not be at all surprised; actually we would be rather pleased to meet one or more of them strolling down Colorado Boulevard!

Though he has been gone for more than two centuries, this is the kind of experience that I relive constantly with one of my musical heroes, Johann Sebastian Bach. Why is this man for me so vital, interesting, so real? Is it because of his musical genius? Yes, one is continually amazed with the prodigious feats of this mental giant in so many areas of musical composition and performance. But, Sebastian Bach pulls at me primarily because of the kind of person he *was*, and not just because of what he *did*. His love for God and a firm religious belief expressed through his music, the pride in his musical ancestry and the fatherly tenderness with which he *cared* for a very large family—his conscientious habits and his insistence upon perfection of detail; these and other similar traits are undeniably positive and admirable. Yet, Bach, like all of us, had his times of discouragement and downright despair. He courted trouble by his seeming inability to speak or to act with diplomacy and kindness. There were quarrels with his colleagues and complaints to those in authority. Unfortunately, he pos-

So it is that in spite of his genius, Bach is enough of an average human being that we have no difficulty in identifying with him. We can sympathize with his anxieties and sorrows and rejoice in his success.

51

sessed a violent temper which often flared out of control. So it is that in spite of his genius, Bach is enough of an average human being that we have no difficulty in identifying with him. We can sympathize with his anxieties and sorrows and rejoice in his success. By accepting his life which in so many respects is contradictory and paradoxical, we may better understand the extent of his greatness.

As one learns the details of his personal life, it seems as though Bach had to endure more than his share of heartbreak. Death took his mother and father when he was only a young boy. His first wife, Barbara, to whom he was devoted, died unexpectedly while he was completing an assignment which had taken him away from home. By her, and with a second marriage to Anna Magdalena, 20 children were born into the Bach household; yet, only seven of these lived to an adult age. This succession of tragic events seemingly would be enough to daunt almost any man.

However, Bach possessed great powers of perseverance. So, he carried on in ways which evidently he thought were right and best for him. He taught four of his sons with such care that three of them eventually became famous as composers and performers throughout the entire European continent. Two of his boys received a thorough training at the University of Leipzig in law, mathematics and philosophy, for their father believed that a man needed a knowledge of these disciplines in order to make a better musician of himself. One may sense Bach's fatherly pride in these lines which he wrote recommending his son, Johann Bernhard, for a position as organist in the little town of Mühlhausen:

> It is reported that Mr. Hetzehenn, Town Organist in Mühlhausen, recently died there, and that his post has to date not been filled. Now, since my youngest son, Johann Gottfried Bernhard Bach, has already acquired such skill in music that I am firmly convinced that he is fully equipped and able to attend to this newly vacated post of town organist; therefore I beg Your Honor, in most grateful deference, to be good enough to give my son the benefit of your highly valued intercession.

Bernhard was given the position but his experience proved to be an unhappy one. Some comments about his playing which were made by the authorities may have a familiar ring for us today. "Young Bach plays far too much—and far too long." And, another voiced his complaints in this fashion: "If Bernhard Bach continues to play in this way, the organ will be ruined in two years, or else most of the congregation will be deaf."

Because of these criticisms, Bernhard pleaded with his father to find him another position. Such was secured in the city of Sangerhausen. Soon, however, the son was responsible for bringing new sorrow to his father. Let this letter written by J.S. Bach tell the story:

With what pain and sorrow, however, I frame this reply, Your Honor can judge for yourself as the loving and well-meaning father of Your Honor's own beloved offspring. Upon my (alas! misguided) son I have not laid eyes since last year, when I had the honor to enjoy many courtesies at Your Honor's hands. Your Honor is also not unaware that at that time I duly paid not only his board but also the Mühlhausen draft (which presumably brought about his departure at that time), but also [*sic*] left a few ducats behind to settle a few bills, in the hope that he would now embark upon a new mode of life. But now I must learn again, with greatest consternation, that he once more borrowed here and there, and did not change his way of living in the slightest, but on the contrary has even absented himself and not given me to date any inkling as to his whereabouts.

What shall I say or do further? Since no admonition, nor even any loving care and *assistance* will suffice any more, I must bear my cross in patience, and leave my unruly son to God's Mercy alone, doubting not that He will hear my sorrowful pleading, and in the end will so work upon him, according to His Holy Will, that he will learn to acknowledge that the lesson is owing wholly and alone to Divine Goodness.

As a young man living today might do in similar circumstances, Johann Sebastian Bach did everything possible to better himself and so to improve his financial position. He changed his place of employment four times. He thought nothing of walking 200 miles in order to see and learn from another great organist. He copied the music of composers whom he admired in order to teach himself the rudiments of Italian and French styles of composition. He sought to be named as a "court composer" by sending to princes and kings examples of his work which had been written especially for their birthday or coronation anniversary celebration. However, Bach never achieved fame as a composer in his own lifetime. Very few of his pieces were published. Rather, it was his remarkable skill as an organist which brought him renown. So—there were those who were his close friends and who paid tribute to his genius—and there were also close at hand those critics who spoke disparagingly of his efforts as teacher and composer and who laughed at "old Bach" as a peculiar and old-fashioned musician.

I like this word picture of Bach's activities as he conducted his musicians. It was written by one of his close friends.

If you could see him, I say, doing what many of your citharoedists and six hundred of your tibia players together could not do, not only, like a citharoedist, singing with one voice and playing his own parts, but watching over everything and bring back to the rhythm and the beat, out of thirty or even forty musicians (*symphoniaci*), the one with a nod, another by tapping with his foot, the third with a warning finger, giving the right note to one from the top of his voice, to another from the bottom, and to a third from the middle of it—all alone, in the midst of the greatest din made by all the participants, and, although he is executing the most difficult parts himself, noticing at once whenever and wher-

Johann Sebastian Bach did everything possible to better himself and so to improve his financial position. He changed his place of employment four times. He thought nothing of walking 200 miles in order to see and to learn from another great organist. He copied the music of composers whom he admired in order to teach himself the rudiments of Italian and French styles of composition.

ever a mistake occurs, holding everyone together, taking precautions everywhere, and repairing any unsteadiness, full of rhythm in every part of his body—this one man taking in all these harmonies with this keen ear and emitting with his voice alone the tone of all the voices. Favorer as I am of antiquity, the accomplishments of Bach, and of any others that there may be like him, appear to me to effect what not many Orpheuses, nor twenty Arions, could achieve.

JOHANN MATTHIAS GESNER

But how Johann Sebastian Bach must have suffered as he read these critical words, from the pen of a young man who had once been one of his favorite students:

I have heard this great man play on various occasions. One is amazed at his ability and one can hardly conceive how it is possible for him to achieve such agility, with his fingers and with his feet, in the crossings, extensions, and extreme jumps that he manages, without mixing in a single wrong tone, or displacing his body by any violent movement.

This great man would be the admiration of whole nations if he had more amenity (*Annehmlichket*), if he did not take away from the natural element in his pieces by giving them a turgid (*schwülstig*) and confused style, and if he did not darken their beauty by an excess of art. Since he judges according to his own fingers, his pieces are extremely difficult to play; for he demands that singers and instrumentalists should be able to do with their throats and instruments whatever he can play on the clavier. But this is impossible.

JOHANN ADOLPH SCHEIBE

We need from time to time to develop a philosophy, a statement of belief—a credo, if you will—concerned with why we do what we do. So I suggest. . . .

Four vital C's, if you please—"Choice, Compromise, Courage, and Confidence"—which must be perfected to become an integral part of the lifestyle of choral conductors who hope for success in musical activity and self-fulfillment in their living.—"Choice, Compromise, Courage, and Confidence: A Choral Credo for the '80s," American Choral Directors Association, Minnesota, 1981.

Bach's fourth and last position was as a church musician in Leipzig where he remained for 27 years. Here he was responsible for planning and performing all of the music for two of the city's churches—St. Thomas—and St. Nicholas—and with the help of assistants he also supervised the music for 2 other congregations. He taught Latin to the boys in the choir school and was responsible for some of their discipline. Bach composed most of the music which was played and sung in the services, taught it to his singers and instrumentalists, conducted its performance, and played the organ. Some idea of the tremendous outpouring of his music may be gathered by learning that in addition to the vast number of his pieces for instruments, Johann Sebastian Bach composed 3 Passion settings, Christmas and Easter oratorios, a *Magnificat*, 4 Lutheran masses and the great *Mass in B Minor*, 6 church motets, and most amazing of all, nearly 300 church cantatas for all of the Sundays and special days of the liturgical year in the Lutheran church.

Bach's state of mind was hardly helped by many of his professional relationships in Leipzig. To begin with, he was the *third choice* of the Town Council for the position of Cantor—the name for the man charged with the responsibilities for the music in the churches. The minutes of their meetings tell of one councilor who made this statement—almost unbelievable to us today. He said, in referring to their

54

choice of Bach, "Since the best man for the post could not be obtained, mediocre ones would have to be accepted." And, this negative attitude continued to exist during the many years that Bach labored in the city. He was charged by the Council with leaving Leipzig without obtaining permission, his teaching was not good, he was "incorrigible," "he showed little inclination to work," and so forth. A quarrel with the Headmaster or Rector of the choir school went on for nearly two years and involved many letters of protest written by Bach to the Council but with no result. He then appealed to the Consistory, which was a body of men representing the Council, the churches, and the university, but they refused to act. Finally, the petition went to the king who insisted that the disagreement between his court composer Bach and the rector be settled once and for all, and it was!

While the reason for the quarrel was a petty one, in all justice it should be said that the animosity between Bach and his rector came about primarily because the rector wished to modernize his school by extending the range of subjects to be studied by the pupils in their music rehearsals. It was reported that when the rector found one lad practicing with his violin he said "So—it is a pothouse fiddler you wish to become!" The students soon learned that their rector considered music to be an inferior kind of occupation.

Yet it must be reported that in the midst of these quarrels—at times our Cantor allowed his temper to get the best of him—he refused to eat with the boys—chased one young man out of the church during a service—and kept sending a stream of letters to the authorities which were filled with harsh statements describing the many negative aspects of his position. Yet, it is a remarkable fact that at the same time that much of this was taking place, Bach was organizing and writing a document which described in remarkable detail the church music situation as he found it in Leipzig. There is time to read only a few lines from this interesting memorandum which carries the title, "Short but most necessary draft for a well-appointed church music; with certain modest reflections on the decline of the same":

> A well-appointed church music requires vocalists and instrumentalists.
>
> The vocalists are in this place made up of the pupils of the Thomas-Schule, being of four kinds, namely, sopranos (*Discantisten*), altos, tenors, and basses ....
>
> Every musical choir should contain at least 3 sopranos, 3 altos, 3 tenors, and as many basses, so that even if one happens to fall ill (as very often happens, particularly at this time of year, as the prescriptions written by the school physician for the apothecary must show) at least a double-chorus motet may be sung

How was Johann Sebastian Bach able to cope with his demanding schedule and with the constant trouble with his superiors? Let his

While Bach's assurance was shaken at times by his very human doubts and fears, there is no question but that his trust in God and in the fudamentals of the Christian faith were all important for his well-being.

works answer the question. On more than one occasion he is reported to have said, "I am obliged to work hard, but whoever is equally industrious will succeed as well as I." And when he was complimented on his artistry in playing the organ he replied, "There is nothing to it. You only have to hit the right notes at the right time and the instrument plays itself!"

While Bach's assurance was shaken at times by his very human doubts and fears, there is no question but that his trust in God and in the fundamentals of the Christian faith were all important for his well-being. He regularly inscribed his scores at their beginnings with the words, "Jesu Juva"—meaning, "Jesus, Help" and at the end with the letters S.D.G. standing for "Soli Deo Gloria"—"to God be the glory." As one contemporary writer has said, "Bach did not shed his religion when he composed either for religious or for other secular purposes. All music was in the service of God."

Bach's interest in religious matters is shown in other ways. He wrote the texts for some of his cantatas. He possessed a good library of books and commentaries on sacred subjects. He took an active interest in some of the theological disputes of his times; at one period he supported publicly a point of view directly opposite to that held by his own pastor. However, as his great biographer, Albert Schweitzer, says,

> Bach's real religion was not orthodox Lutheranism, but mysticism. In his innermost essence he belongs to the history of German mysticism. This robust man, who seems to be in the thick of life with his family and his work, and whose mouth seems to express something like comfortable joy in life, was inwardly dead to the world. His whole thought was transfigured by a wonderful, serene longing for death.

An astonishing number of the cantatas composed by Bach speak eloquently of his steadfast faith and hope for the future. One of the greatest of these we are to hear this morning. "Christ Lay in the Bonds of Death" is not the usual kind of music we expect to hear performed at Easter time. It does not contain passages of exuberant joy—one will not listen to bells and trumpets—harps and drums. Rather, the *two* great events of Passion Week are described in mystical and philosophical terms. To put it as simply as possible, the cantata depicts the struggle between Death and the Resurrection with the latter winning a most glorious victory.

I will not speak at length about the cantata; in a few minutes the music will tell its own story. But here are a few points of interest. The melody of the choral goes back to the 12th century. Martin Luther revised it—wrote all of the words of the text, and it appeared in the first Lutheran hymnal published in 1524—exactly 455 years ago. Bach composed this cantata in an interesting fashion. Each of the seven sections or movements of the work correspond to the seven hymn verses as written by Luther. But, Bach uses musical ideas from the hymn so

56

that each of the seven verses is quite different from the other and yet we are always aware of the hymn or chorale. Also, the composer shows us how fond he is of logic and design in writing his music. The movements are arranged symmetrically; that is, the first chorus balances with the last chorale. The second and sixth movements are duets; the third and fifth are solos sung by the entire sections in the choir, and the center movement is a great chorus which depicts the battle between Death and Life in graphic sounds. (As was true in Bach's time, we are going to ask the congregation to participate in this presentation by singing the chorale both at the beginning and the end of the cantata. Anita Priest will indicate when you are to sing.)

And, as you listen to this music today, think of its creator, Johann Sebastian Bach. Knowing so well both joy and sorrow, longing for death but living each day conscientiously, poor in this world's resources but rich in family and friends, human in his errors and great in his genius: this was J. S. Bach. I will not meet him on Colorado Boulevard, but it is not impossible to imagine that at times he is peering over my shoulder as I conduct one of his compositions. All who will listen with appreciation to his music can sense the spirit of this man whose faith in God was unshakeable and everlasting.

Knowing so well both joy and sorrow, longing for death but living each day conscientiously, poor in this world's resources but rich in family and friends, human in his errors and great in his genius: this was J. S. Bach.

Why Art?

In this 1985 address at the Plymouth Congregational Church in Des Moines, Iowa, Swan answers the basic question "Why music in a service of worship?"

I remember well my first day as a tenth grader in a high school journalism class. The teacher explained that in writing about any event a reporter always should include in the first paragraph brief answers for these questions: *what* was the incident or experience; *who* were the participants; *how* and *when* and *where* did the event take place; and finally, *why* was this particular incident so important that it deserved to be mentioned in the Hollywood High School student newspaper? Sometimes it was quite difficult to find an explanation for the *why* because this depended upon the personal and subjective opinions of the reporter. This is true for almost any area of inquiry. It is not easy to find answers for this particular question. *Why* art? *Why* music? Why use music in a service of worship?

What do we mean when we use the word "art"? If this question was to be asked of each of you, quite possibly there would be as many answers as there are people in attendance here this morning. However, the dictionary can help us. Do you like this statement? "(Art is) the conscious production or arrangement of sounds, colors, forms, movements or other elements in a manner that affects the sense of *beauty*." If there is this close relationship between art and what is beautiful, what then is *beauty*? Again we may turn to a dictionary for guidance. We are told that "beauty is an *appearance* or *sound* that arouses a strong, contemplative delight." And, this following definition is perhaps the most helpful. "Beauty is a pleasing quality associated with harmony of form or color, excellence of craftsmanship, truthfulness, originality, or other unspecifiable property."

Why *art*? If art is beauty, if it has quality, if it is pleasing as to form or color—is excellent in its rendition or execution, if art involves self-expression and many times will develop individual creativity and originality, if above all its representation bears the marks of integrity; if all of these factors compose that which we call "art"—it follows that we should understand and appreciate every manifestation of the artistic. For, who is there who will condemn beauty?

Music is one branch of the arts. Herbert Spencer probably was indulging in flights of fancy when he declared that "music must take rank as the highest of the fine arts, as the one which more than any

If we can agree that all art is expressive, if it can be symbolic, association, beautiful, if it pictures in form and color or sound man's highest thought and aspiration, then art surely belongs in the church. And this is true of music.

other ministers to human welfare." I'm not sure that music deserves such commendation. However, I have witnessed wonderful things happening to individuals of all ages when they have possessed voices and have used them in singing with a choir or chorus. If they are privileged to work with a leader who combines fine musicianship with an ability to communicate effectively with the singers, each chorister has the opportunity to live for a period with greatness as expressed by the two originators of the related arts of poetry and musical composition.

Art is expressive. If one sings or paints, or acts, or plays an instrument, or writes poetry, or sketches plans for a great new building, something goes from the creator into that which he or she has created. And we cannot rest until others have seen or heard what we have done and have recognized our work. When we speak of music I like to compare this process with the shape of a triangle.

If we can agree that all art is expressive, if it can be symbolic, associational, beautiful, if it pictures in form and color or sound man's highest thought and aspiration, then *art* surely belongs in the church. And this is true of music.

Church? What is its function? First, there is the sense of fellowship—of community—as we sing together our great hymns. Also, we use this honorable art to create atmosphere, to heighten a mood, to strengthen the attributes of awe, mystery, penitence, and praise—elements accepted in most quarters as necessary for a successful worship experience. Music has one of its functions here in Plymouth Church, the bringing to a worshipper's attention a subject or theme or purpose which then has its development in the sermon of the minister. Finally, music together with all other forms of art which are used in worship should be considered as a sacrifice—as an act of stewardship—one way by which we glorify God. I like this statement of Archibald Davison: "There is but one great purpose for which church music may be employed, and that is to the glory of God; not for any of the psychological, social and utilitarian ends to which our worship music is now tortured out of its true nature, but as an *offering*, a sacrifice, a return in kind of God's gift of beauty to man." Why is it that we insist on building splendid edifices in which to worship—we possess beautiful paintings and sculptures and exquisite stained glass windows—but (and surely this does not apply to Plymouth Church!) we are content with an inferior brand of church music? So many persons insist upon hearing a kind of music which makes them "feel good," sets their toes to tapping, is overly sentimental, and does not attempt to be something of quality. Rather, this music is judged as to its *entertainment* value; whether its sound measures up to what is heard in the shopping mall, the bank, or on TV!

Music must assume a greater potential than to be merely a device which makes one comfortable. If we can bring the best that we have in music to God as a sacrifice—an offering—then this becomes truly a part of our worship experience. Through inspired music we praise and pray and preach. With the prophet Isaiah we can answer the question, "Who will go for us?" "Here am I, send me!"

If we can bring the best that we have in music to God as a sacrifice—an offering— then this becomes truly a part of our worship experience. Through inspired music we praise and pray and preach. With the prophet Isaiah we can answer the question, "Who will go for us?" "Here am I, send me?"

61

3
Credo:
The Conductor

Style, Performance Practice and Choral Tone

In this article, requested by the California Music Educators Association for inclusion in their newsletter and subsequently published in the November/December 1965 issue, Swan discusses the importance of these three aspects of conducting and teaching.

This is the decade when choral conductors are becoming familiar with the terms "musical style" and "performance practice." They understand that only those men and women who possess a proper kind of musical information will be able to secure a valid interpretation from their choruses. These will be the artists—the intuitive conductors among us.

At the present time directors are busily engaged in learning all that is possible about "style." This is a worthwhile enterprise. For too long this area of knowledge has been neglected in the training and knowledge of those who lead singers. In the nineteen thirties the director of choral music was forced to concentrate upon finding a repertoire for his chorus. Suitable materials were scarce. The next period in our comparatively brief choral history found the conductor busy with other matters: rehearsal techniques, organizational procedures and the development of a beautiful tone. So it is that the concern for a proper choral rendition stylistically speaking, is almost a contemporary matter.

Only a person bereft of his senses would argue that study of the several periods of musical composition is a waste of time. The varying nature of historical composition is a reflection of the social, political, religious and artistic environment in which great composers worked and lived. Their writing was conditioned by the musical knowledge of their times and by the vocal and instrumental forces that were available for their use. That a person who proposes to recreate in sound the original idea of a great composer should know how to read his language, to study his score—almost goes without saying.

Unfortunately, with our American penchant for placing ideas in neat little categories we are now busily and happily engaged in building our lists of style characteristics. Almost any conductor can recite those stylistic factors which he expects to find in a score written during the Renaissance or in the baroque or in the classic, romantic and con-

While we learn slowly but somewhat surely that the secret of a proper choral interpretation lies in understanding the individual score, conductors as a group are doing almost nothing towards solving the difficult problems which center about the term "performance practice."

temporary periods of composition. If the score in question does not seem to "fit," it receives a standard "historical" stylistic treatment complete with flourishes. Sometimes there seems to be no consideration of *where* the composer lived (nationalistic and economic factors) or *when* (early or late) he worked within a given period, or most importantly, *how* his writing may be compared stylistically and technically with others who were his contemporaries.

The difficulty here is that we expect a set of rules to care for all matters of interpretation for those composers who happen to be born within a chronological period of time. Such a list of characteristics never can take the place of a careful reading which leads to the understanding and appreciation of the individual score. Palestrina did not write as did Victoria. All Bach's compositions are alike in some respects, but they differ in many others. To move towards an "authentic" rendering of a Haydn piece so that it doesn't sound like Brahms or Schubert is a great step forward, but it is not enough. Who wishes to listen to a set of madrigals written by different composers if each selection sounds exactly like all of the others?

While we learn slowly but somewhat surely that the secret of a proper choral interpretation lies in understanding the individual score, conductors as a group are doing almost nothing towards solving the difficult problems which center about the term "performance practice." All authorities agree that the recreation of an authentic performance, that is, the presentation of a piece as the composer originally intended or as it was done for the first time, is impossible to do today. Too often, however, we disregard features of performance which *are* possible of accomplishment and which would give to the music a sound much closer to that pictured by the composer.

There is no doubt that much early music should be performed by a group which is small in size. The phrasing, the texture, and the line all call for a limited number of voices. Do we bear this in mind as we choose chorus personnel? Much of this same music demands the use of instruments either to support or to replace the voice parts. Yet some are so wedded to the "ideal" of an a cappella tone that they cannot bring themselves to perform the music in any other fashion. In annual *Messiah* presentations the bulky choruses, slow tempos, improper instrumentation and ostentatious and romantic solo singing do a grave injustice to a great composer who is largely unappreciated because his music has not been properly heard. Robert Donington puts it, "Because we perform Handel so much we think that we are performing him traditionally."

Important factors relating to style and interpretation eventually can be found after a proper study of the score. Musicologists give valuable help to the conductor who desires to make his performances authentic. However, there is one problem familiar to all of us which affects and in turn will be influenced by the singing of any piece. I speak of the production and development of a choral tone.

It is rather astounding to discover among contemporary conductors who work in this country and in Europe very little agreement as to the relative importance of the kind of tone produced by their choruses. Presumably there should be some form of logic in the proposition that an inexperienced singer must be taught the correct way to use his instrument. He "plays" it at the same time that he is attempting to build its potential. Yet there are those, and the number is not few, who claim with some complacency that the demands of the score will bring out that in the voice which is needed for a suitable vocal interpretation. One sings a score after being instructed how to do so, and presto—he is endowed with a satisfactory instrument!

On the other hand there are those who worship at the shrine of choral tone. Their own particular brand possesses *the* perfect quality. It is the result of days and months of repetitious and monotonous drill. All matters of interpretation are subservient to the demands of a unique tonal production. Differences in compositions including stylistic factors are colored by a tone which must remain relatively constant because the choir has been taught to produce it at all times. For the conductor who works in this fashion, differences in musical style are not nearly as important as the necessity to produce his "ideal" tone.

But, do all conductors agree as to an ideal tone? For that matter, is there agreement among singers or teachers of singing, or audiences who listen? I think not. To be sure, all of us ask for a tone which is not breathy, which possesses some resonance and which is sung to the center of a pitch. At this point we leave our pleasant unanimity. We are not alike in our ideas of an emphasis dynamics, vibrato rate, matter of attack and release, balance, color of pronunciation, definition of "placement," of "register," and a host of other pertinent factors. This disagreement in the ranks is one reason why any chorus has a different sound from any other group.

This is not the place to discuss or to analyze the several techniques by which we may develop choral tone. Rather, I would suggest that in making the choice of the sound which we wish to hear from our choirs we are forced also to choose the style of music which they can sing most effectively.

Many groups in the United States are led by those who prefer a choral tone which might be described as big, dark, lush, and capable of reproduction at a dynamic level ranging from *mp* to *fff*. The individual vibrato (not tremolo) is encouraged because it is believed that a mature sound results. Is there any doubt that a chorus trained to sing with this tone will be most successful in its rendition of pieces written by nineteenth century composers where subjective color and broad dynamic contrast are a vital necessity? But how effective can this chorus

We will conduct more effectively if we accept the promise that there will be a strong relationship between the tone used by our singers and the kind of music which we like best to hear them sing.

sing sacred polyphony when the emphasis must be upon the impersonal and the blending out of the individual voice?

What of the choir that is taught to use *mf* as its loudest possible dynamic? Usually such a group also sings with a beautiful blend because great stress is laid upon a unified pronunciation. With these characteristics as fundamental in their tone, a choir will reproduce beautifully most compositions of the Renaissance. Yet it cannot possibly be as convincing as it sings music representative of other periods of history.

A conductor who teaches his chorus to sing with an artificial and pseudo rhythmic vitality may excite audiences with his folk music but never will be able to reproduce properly the Bach line. A dynamic balance which is evenly distributed throughout the choir works for most music but not for some romantic compositions or for a baroque piece which calls for the increased importance of the bass. A "heavy" tone is hardly adequate for Mozart. Even those directors who insist upon a certain rigidity in the articulation of consonants create phrasing difficulties with some music which are almost impossible to overcome.

Are there choruses who can change their tone at will to correspond with the interpretive demands of a composition? Perhaps a group of professional singers can do this. Most of us must continue to make choices—not only of the repertoire and of the music which we like best (and which we usually conduct best) but of the kind of tone which we enjoy hearing from our chorus. We will conduct more effectively if we accept the premise that there will be a strong relationship between the tone used by our singers and the kind of music which we like best to hear them sing.

Choral Tradition and the Choral Sound

This October 17, 1966 lecture/demonstration utilized the Occidental Glee Clubs for the purpose of exploring artistry and style in ensemble singing.

Some words are almost never mentioned these days within the environment of a college. *Tradition* is one of these. To suggest that there is an established pattern, an orderly procedure, a traditional way to perform, calls forth a response which often is skeptical and at best is disinterested. A positive answer frequently appears as a proposal to replace the old by something sure to be better because it is new.

Yet, the title of this address implies that there *is* a choral tradition. For singing is the oldest form of musical expression. There has been time to refine the techniques of choral composition and performance. Composers have written some of their greatest masterpieces for voices and tradition, together with style and artistry is an attribute of good singing.

But, do artistry and style and tradition always accompany performance? I think not. It must be confessed that singers sometimes are considered a breed apart by other musicians who are critical of vocal technique and accomplishment. For while a vast number of singers have profited by a musical experience, their pleasure in participation is one paradoxical reason why some choirs fail to reach a point of artistic excellence. In the opinion of many, the folk element from which the choral art draws much of its life and substance establishes arbitrary limits for technical excellence. Unfortunately, it is easy to sing, but difficult to sing well.

From earliest times choral music has been identified with the church and the school. As these institutions have prospered, so has ensemble singing. But, this association has been a mixed blessing. On the one hand the relationship has resulted in a veritable flood of literature including masterpieces which are the product of sheer genius. Yet, the presentation of an authentic performance of this early music, a reproduction in sound of the composer's ideas, is impossible. The notation of the score cannot tell us exactly how to perform the piece. The composition may demand the use of instruments which today are obsolete. Because of the complex requirements of performance, the

In the opinion of many, the folk element from which the choral art draws much of its life and substance establishes arbitrary limits for technical excellence. Unfortunately, it is easy to sing, but difficult to sing well.

69

interpreter not only is a musician, but social historian, theologian, poet and phonetician as well.

During some earlier periods of music history a composer was also a performer and wrote for himself and his own requirements. Because he was knowledgeable in areas of composition and performance he was expected to defend his ideas with his pen. Contrast this with the processes of specialization as they operate today. Musical scholars argue the technical details of a score with only a secondary interest in its proper sound. On the other hand, the performer—in this case a choral conductor—too often does not understand or is not interested in the content of any musicological conversation.

Yet, in spite of waste and war, sputnik and science, taxes and television, these could be magnificent years for for the choral art as for all forms of musical expression. When judged solely by interest and activity, this country appears to be musically supreme. While making a survey of the European choral scene three years ago, I was asked many times about my desire to hear the representative choirs in Britain and on the continent. Why had I traveled such a distance? Did I not know that the very best choruses and orchestras now were to be found in America?

Yes, there is interest in choral music. Never before has there been such good literature to sing, and a considerable amount of this material carries the imprimatur of an editor who is also a scholar. Demands of church and school have combined to create a host of choruses composed of singers of every age and level of ability. Colleges and universities develop courses of study for the training of the potential conductor and professional societies exist for the exchange of ideas among the members of the choral fraternity. Symphony orchestras sponsor their own choral units, and a half-dozen professional choirs exercise a remarkable influence upon the standards of American choral performance with their recordings and concert presentations.

Musical activity in America is remarkable. But, what of musical artistry? What of tradition? For it is essential that a choral tradition is the result of efforts which are both scholarly and technical. A conductor who is familiar with the techniques of singing can draw from his choir a sound which is both beautiful and impressive. Since the human instrument does not come ready equipped to play upon, the building of such a sound is not an easy task. Procedures relating to the support of tone, proper blend and balance, diction and phrasing, legato line, rhythmic precision, clean voweling, and disciplined articulation— these have had to be the concern of conductors who consider themselves masters of their profession. These methods must be taught; the good conductor always is a good teacher.

But, if there are choruses which demonstrate technical mastery, why do we not hear from them a series of performances which are art-

Without affection and respect communication fails. So many times in the very make-up of our rehearsals we provide for the antithesis of communication. We stand on our podium, or on a box; we really say to our group, "Look at me, I am great, I know more than you, I'm not going to tell you all that I know because you have to grow up to that. If you're good boys and girls when you are seniors I'll let you know what I'm thinking about." **"Symposium Summary, Observations and Reflections,"** *Southwestern Musician,* **December 1977.**

70

istically satisfying? Why is it that most choirs sound much the same whether they sing Bach or Palestrina or Brahms? Why are there so few truly great choruses? If there is a choral tradition, and by this we mean a performance of the score which is faithful to the original concepts of the composer, how is this attained, and when are we sure that we have it?

It seems to me that a satisfying interpretation of a choral score depends upon three factors. First, the conductor appraises the technical resources of his instrument (the chorus) and accepts its limitations together with the capacity to learn how to sing well. Second, the director understands the score from the standpoint of its structural and formal detail and is well acquainted with the writing style of the man who wrote it. Finally, the conductor evaluates those personal traits or characteristics within himself which influence the singing of his chorus. Not only are these factors musical but are emotional and aesthetic as well. That rare conductor who succeeds in becoming an artist is almost intuitive as he works with these three basic requirements for

Howard Swan, front row center, director of The University Glee Club of Los Angeles, 1934

The University Glee Club of Los Angeles.

71

interpretive success: He understands his score, his instrument and himself.

Any series of assumptions demands some measure of proof. With music such must be determined subjectively, for judgments are made according to what we hear. Before the evening is over I will conduct a rehearsal which will allow you to make your own interpretation of interpretive phenomena. However, it is necessary at this point to speak briefly of the problem of authenticity as it relates to the recreation of a musical score.

Music is sound in motion in time. It does not exist in space as do literature, art and architecture. Therefore, each succeeding rendition of a particular score by the same group will possess some degree of difference in performance. It follows that every rehearsal and performance of the same score is new. Since a composition will be sung or played countless numbers of times it is not possible always to capture that unique and particular sound or effect which the composer had in mind as he wrote. Nor is this the only difficulty. Much of the great choral music was written during a period of history when composers did not give detailed directions for its performance. They expected the singers to add to the score—to take liberties with it, to improvise and to embellish; in short, to read between the lines and to know when such additions would be both effective and tasteful. A kind of intuition is demanded of the contemporary conductor; he makes his educated guesses concerning interpretive detail, and these must have their foundation in scholarly judgment.

An authentic performance becomes a problem when a composer has written for instruments which today either no longer exist or must be played with a specialized skill possessed by only a few individuals. Another problem arises because composers of the older music wrote for a particular group or had in mind a specific place for performance. Since Bach composed many of his pieces for the choir of St. Thomas in Leipzig and Monteverdi for the great Venetian Cathedral of San Marco, since Haydn had the chapel of the Esterhazys in mind and Palestrina the Vatican choir—how can any contemporary performance reproduce the physical and acoustical and personal characteristics of the groups and the places with which these composers were familiar?

Still one other matter concerned with authenticity needs our attention. Dare we attempt to leap over the hurdle of two of three hundred years which lie between the time of original composition and contemporary performance? Can we listen with the same kind of understanding and appreciation as those who first heard the early music, or will it sound strange and unusual to us? To say it simply—do the factors which constitute the authentic in a musical score tend to disrupt communication between a choir and its audience? What is aesthetically acceptable for twentieth-century audiences? One answer might proceed in this fashion: "We know that Bach wrote many of his major works for a choir of 17 singers and an orchestra of 18 players. His soprano and alto sections were composed principally of little boys. These scanty forces were all that were available for his use. We know also that Bach's great contemporary, G.F. Handel, was unfamiliar with some of our modern instruments for they had not yet been invented. But, if Bach or Handel or any other composer of early music had been given the opportunity to work with 100 voices or had known the instrumentation of our contemporary orchestras, they would have composed music to utilize these resources. Therefore it follows that we should not be the least bit concerned with changing our performance practices if the sound which results will be more acceptable to the audience."

This opinion is popular in many places. So we listen and praise the lush versions of the *Messiah* which have been recreated by Thomas Beecham and Leonard Bernstein. We applaud unaccompanied renditions of music which were scored originally for voices and instruments, some to supplement and others to take the place of voices. We applaud because we enjoy the "pretty" sound of voices singing without instrumental support—and you may believe that the conductor of the choir is applauding silently with his audience.

A few seasons ago Thomas Dunn, a young and talented New York conductor, performed the Bach *Mass in B Minor* patterned as closely as possible after the manner that J. S. Bach presented his music each Sunday in St. Thomas church. The instrumentation, the number of participants and the interpretive ideas were as faithful to the score as was possible. Most scholars, some colleagues and the discriminating audience cheered this brave try for authenticity in performance. On the other hand, Harold Shoenberg, the critic of the *New York Times*, was scornful. He said in part, "Regardless of what Bach used because he had to, large forces appear implicit in the nature of his writing. 'Large,' of course is a relative term, but the great movements of the *B Minor Mass* and the *St. Matthew Passion* and other equivalent works surely demand a volume of tone grander than the pipings and squeakings of a chorus of eight, or twelve, or even twenty. Bach must have had an enormous sound in his inner ear when he penned those sublime notes or else internal evidence means nothing." Mr. Schoenberg might have paraphrased his remarks in this fashion: Why try to reproduce the 18th century in the midst of the twentieth when a perfect reproduction is both unknowable and impossible?

Mr. Schoenberg is correct in his conclusion that a completely authentic performance is *not* possible. It is difficult to recover what in many instances is almost a lost tradition and often we are unable to apply the tradition even if we know what it is. But, in spite of the necessity for compromise, is not the performer obligated to keep striving

Dare we attempt to leap over the hurdle of two or three hundred years which lie between the time of the original composition and contemporary performance? Can we listen with the same kind of understanding and appreciation as those who first heard the early music, or will it sound strange and unusual to us?

73

towards the ideal? Should he not continue the attempt to discover what the composer had in mind as he wrote his music? Can a conductor ignore the important contribution which his own scholarship will make to a performance of integrity and taste? As Donald Grout puts it, "The only danger in one's ability to develop an ideal performance would seem to be that it could mislead one into regarding knowledge of the past as a substitute for imagination in the present rather than as food for it."

But you would be amazed to know the number of conductors who take exception to Mr. Grout's statement. These men see no merit in working with vocal methods or techniques and are not particularly interested in tone. Rather, the score is all important. If its intricacies are resolved, very little else needs doing. It is almost as though the music becomes the teacher—its demands call forth from the singer an appropriate response and the ability to master any technical difficulty. Yet, if one is to judge by their performances some of these directors do not hear sound mentally as they prepare their scores. They will not accept the premise that choral sound must be developed beginning with the very first rehearsal because of its relationship to all other technical and interpretive aspects of the music. They believe instead that nothing need be done about tone except to make sure that the score is sung correctly. This process is assumed to guarantee automatically the appropriate sound.

When a director relies upon his knowledge of the score to solve all choral problems, his study moves through definite procedural patterns. First, there is the understanding of style characteristics which are representative of any historical period of composition. All pieces of music which have been written during a particular period of time will reflect some common stylistic tendencies. The next step is to identify those devices which are unique in the writing of a particular composer. Finally, each individual score must be examined to learn its specific requirements; that is, How do two works written by the same composer differ from each other? Complete understanding comes only after a study of the composer's ancestry, nationality, environment, training, and the original purpose for which the composition was written. One needs to know *why* the man wrote as he did; the *how* is not sufficient for a faithful interpretation.

In direct contrast to the man who believes that a musical composition somehow possesses the power to solve all vocal and interpretive problems is the conductor whose emphasis is on those factors which are related to sound. Unfortunately, he fools his audiences as well as himself because both respond only to aesthetic elements in the music. Now, this director is quite aware of the changes which have taken place in musical composition over the years. But, he isn't interested or does not have the time for intensive study. Perhaps he is lazy. Sometimes he

If a conductor can bring out the force of the human personality of his singers, presuming technically they're capable, it's like firecrackers. If harnessed and brought out, the human personality is so powerful.— "The Editor Interviews . . . Howard Swan," *The Journal of Choral Conductor's Guild,* **February 1970.**

74

is a collector—a collector of lists of style characteristics formulated by some eminent musical authority. With these lists our conductor feels that he is well equipped interpretively—that he can become the master of any score. He applies these characteristics, sometimes quite indiscriminately to any score written in a particular period. Then, he is finished with style and with a consideration of the appropriate methods for performance. He spends his time with his favorite techniques—in particular, with those methods which will draw from his choirs a sound, a tone which perhaps is his trademark with colleagues and listeners.

It seems as though some American musicians believe that rules or lists can care for any problem. This observation was impressed upon me by an incident which took place during the course of a European trip several years ago. My principal objective was to talk to conductors relative to problems of style and interpretation. I was particularly anxious to meet with the director of the Netherlands Chamber Choir and finally found him serving as an adjudicator for the International Eisteddfod in Wales. No sooner had I asked my first question than he exploded: "Ah, you Americans! You think that an answer for every problem is to be found on a certain page of a particular book. When will you learn that it takes a lifetime of study to know how to conduct properly a chorus?"

Eventually, of course, he relaxed and we enjoyed a stimulating discussion. But I have never forgotten the force, and perhaps the truth, of his first ejaculation.

Thus far, my statement has been concerned with the dual relationship between choral tradition and choral sound. I have tried to say that too few choral performances are artistically satisfying. This is because the conductor either does not want to distinguish between composers or periods of composition or else devotes all of his time to musicological phenomena and very little to vocal technique. While a completely faithful representation in sound of the early music is impossible, it is the responsibility of the performer to stay as closely as he is able to the ideas of the composer. A tradition develops only when the conductor (1) is a student of the music and its composer, (2) understands how and when to work with technical elements which are vital to the recreative process in sound, and (3) accepts the importance of his own influence upon the singing of his choirs. This last is stimulated by his gestures, his phraseology and other physical and emotional factors which reflect his musical personality. If any one of these three functional responsibilities is neglected, the performance is a failure.

Now we are ready to conduct a rehearsal. What will be the result when important musical techniques are stressed or omitted? How will this affect your appreciation and standards for judgment? We will fol-

A tradition develops only when the conductor (1) is a student of the music and its composer, (2) understands how and when to work with technical elements which are vital to the recreative process in sound, and (3) accepts the importance of his own influence upon the singing of his choirs.

low this procedure. The Glee Clubs will sing parts of three pieces of early music. Each one will be practiced, first with the emphasis upon the score as a basis for interpretation—second, with the primary objective the development of choral tone. As the rehearsal progresses, I will explain our objectives.

The first number which we will sing is a setting of the *Sanctus* from the mass *Aeterna Christi Munera* by Palestrina. The music is called "polyphonic"—*many voiced*—and, literally there is no one melody or voice part which is more important than any other. One part may be more prominent than the other three for just an instant, and then it is the turn of another, and then another, and another. Because this is true, this music is called "linear." It flows horizontally, and we hear it this way, not as we would hear music written vertically or in a chordal fashion.

[*Accompanist demonstrates chordal and linear styles.*]

Another characteristic of polyphonic music is its use of the principle of *imitation*. One voice section sings a phrase composed of a series of notes of differing pitches and time values. Another voice section will imitate exactly all or part of the phrase, although the *imitators* may begin at a pitch that is lower or higher than the original.

[*Sections of the choir perform imitative excerpts.*]

Palestrina, like all other composers of polyphony, wrote music which had a kind of rhythm, but not as we think of rhythm today. Polyphonic music is not metrical. Metrical or metered music is divided into units of time called measures or bars and each of these contains not only the same number of beats but regularly recurring accents.

[*Performers contrast metered and unmetered music utilizing a march, a waltz, and excerpts from the Palestrina.*]

We have been talking about three elements of style which are basic to all polyphonic compositions: (1) the inclusion of many melodies which are composed in a linear rather than a chordal fashion, (2) the principle of *imitation*, and (3) the absence of a regularly recurring accent. Some other important style characteristics of this period are these: Polyphonic music is *modal*—not written in one of our contemporary keys. While the music and text complement each other, the relationship is one of accent rather than one of literal meaning. For the most part, this kind of music moves *stepwise* rather than using wide intervals or variations in pitch.

But many conductors because of ignorance or inertia concern themselves only with these three principles as they attempt to interpret polyphony. They will say to their choruses, as I now say to the Glee Clubs, "Remember, now, to listen to each other, for no one voice section must be prominent in singing polyphony. The bar lines in your score are only placed there for your convenience in reading music, do not accent the notes which follow the bar lines. Do not overlook the points of imitation in the piece."

[*Remarks following the presentation of a portion of the* Sanctus.]

Would you agree that our singing is rather dull and lifeless? Why? Perhaps it is because we have not acquainted ourselves with the unique musical qualities of this particular composition. The understanding of a few general style characteristics is helpful, but this will not solve all of our problems. Let us look further. For example, Palestrina wrote this *Sanctus* as a setting of a *Latin* text. We have been using the English. Listen while the Glee Clubs sing several phrases of the music— first in the English—and then with the use of the Latin.

[*Remarks following the performance of selected phrases.*]

When the Latin is used the phrases begin and end at different points in the score than when the piece is sung in English. This is a result of poor editing; the editor has altered Palestrina's music so that it will "fit" the English and by doing so has changed the form and structure of the music. You heard also a considerable difference in tone color, in sound, as the singers used the English and then the Latin. But this change in tone is not nearly as important or as serious a matter as the deliberate alteration of the music. When the pitch rises in music, energy is accumulated; and when it descends, energy is dispersed. Therefore, it makes a very great difference *where* in the music the lines begin and end their rise and fall.

Now, for another point. At what speed should this music be sung? Palestrina has not told us; he knew nothing of a metronome or tempo markings. Does this speed seem right to you? [*Glee Clubs sing "too slowly."*] Now, let us try something different. [*Sing "too rapidly."*] Now, for a third attempt. [*Sing with a "normal" speed.*] Most of you probably preferred our last try to the first two. Why? Perhaps, because the tempo allowed the Glee Clubs to sing rapidly enough so that the phrases did not fall apart, and slowly enough so that the succession of notes did not sound hurried or rushed.

[*Demonstration of tempo changes in awkward spots*]

When a chorus departs from a strict tempo, there must be an important reason for doing so. In polyphonic music there are points where this can be done. [*Illustrate.*] This number is constructed sectionally. We should have learned this at the beginning of our score study. How are these sections found? At certain points the phrases change; they become shorter or longer, or they proceed to higher or lower pitches. Note values become longer or shorter. Sometimes, the composer calls for different combinations of voices.

Thus far we have used only two illustrative examples that one must go *beyond* general or *period* characteristics to the individual score in order to determine its proper interpretation. We have talked about the use of English or Latin and the problem of tempo. If more

If the altos are to imitate the sopranos and the tenors and the basses are to follow their example, this means that every individual in each voice section must a.) pronounce each sound exactly like all of his fellow singers, b.) sing with the same degree of loudness and softness as the others in the choir, c.) phrase together. These three objectives take much time to learn.

time were available the score of this *Sanctus* would show us many other pertinent considerations. However, we now must deal with the factors which deal directly with our instrument—the voices of the singers. The problems were perceived originally in their *visual* form in the score—they must be solved with the use of *vocal* techniques. Because voices respond differently to varied stimuli, it is most important that the conductor choose the exercise or technique which will add the proper *aural* validity to the performance.

We spoke a few moments ago of *imitation*. If the altos are to imitate the sopranos and the tenors and the basses are to follow their example, this means that every individual in each voice section must: a.) pronounce each sound exactly like all of his fellow singers, b.) sing with the same degree of loudness and softness as the others in the choir, c.) phrase together. These three objectives take much time to learn. They must be practiced. Because every voice is different, a good conductor is also one who understands singing technique and particularly the way in which a uniformity of tone is gained. To give you some concept of the problems faced by a director, listen to some of the individual voices in the Glee Club ensemble.

[*Illustration with vowel sounds, particularly oo; showing the upper voices of men and the lower voices of women; different vibrato rates and tonal colors; dynamics and blend, etc.*]

"Blend" is the process by which all voices begin to sound as one. You will hear that blend is much more effective when the voices sing softer and when they use the "oo" vowel. Furthermore, the quieter tone makes the women's voices sound somewhat like those of little boys and this, of course, is the sound that Palestrina had in mind as he wrote his motets and masses. The polyphonic style of composition requires a chorus which sings with a beautiful blend; no individual voice should be heard at any time. There is a relationship here also to the theology of the times as expressed in the texts set by polyphonic composers. Although some variation exists from piece to piece, you do not hear from these composers a sobbing *Agnus Dei* or a jubilant *Gloria* or an impassioned *Credo*. We have instead the serenity of a composer who is confident that his setting of a prayer of his church to her God already has been answered.

With the use of these several vocal techniques, perhaps we have developed a polyphonic tone which seems to cope with all stylistic problems in a score—whether these relate to imitation or texture, to the absence of heavy beats, the flow of the linear line or almost any other difficulty which may present itself in this music. Yet, we cannot be sure that we are right. There were no recordings that were made in the 15th or 16th century. Few theorists reported on the sounds which they heard sung by the choirs of their day. One man, a contemporary composer and theorist, Herman Finck, is helpful to us. In a treatise written in 1556, he presented his reaction to the vocal practices of the time. Concerning *blend*, Finck says:

> The treble (the soprano) should be sung with a delicate tone, the bass, however, with a harder and heavier tone; the middle voices should move with uniformity and try to match themselves to the outer parts sweetly and harmoniously. A constant dynamic level should be maintained throughout the composition so that there is no discrepancy in sound between the beginning and the end; the tone should not be too soft or too loud, but rather like a properly built organ the ensemble should remain unaltered and constant.

From time to time Finck describes some of the performances which he has heard: "No one part should ever stand out more than is proper nor should the singers even make such an exertion or articulation of the voice that many of them call attention to themselves by changing color, getting black in the face or running out of breath." He has frequently been present "when fine compositions were monstrously distorted or deformed, with mouths twisted and wide open, heads thrown back and shaking, the singers suffering from the delusion that shouting is the same thing as singing. The basses make a rumbling noise like a hornet trapped in a boot or else expel their breath with a solar eruption and so deprive the composition of its elegance, sweetness and grace. Instead of this, one should use a quality of voice which is sweet, smooth, and polished." All parts are equally important, says Finck, "the higher a voice rises, the quieter and more gentle should be the tone; the lower it goes the richer should be the sound. Each voice should sound just as clear and gentle as any other."

Listen to what Finck has to say concerning the practice of imitation:

> When there is a tasteful point of imitation it should be rendered with a more definite and distinct tone of voice than is employed elsewhere and the following parts if they start with the same point as the first, should perform it in the same way.

Finck's statement seems to substantiate our ideas concerning the interpretation of polyphony. Evidently he believed in blend, in an exact balance of voices at the points of imitation, in moderate and steady tempos and in a tone production if we may call it such, which was quiet and restrained rather than strong and vigorous. We will now use most of these concepts in the interpretation of another composition which comes out of the sixteenth century—the *O Magnum Mysterium* by the Spaniard, Thomas Luis de Victoria. You will hear imitation, linear movement and lack of regular accent in this piece as was true for the *Sanctus*. But you will hear also sounds which are different. This score has more changes of pitch, a greater variety in the length of phrases, and an unusual text. Because he chose a verse like this one, it is safe to assume that Victoria composed his music with its meaning in mind:

O Wondrous Mystery! The Mystery that saw even the animals worshipping at the birth of our Lord. O blessed Virgin who carried our Lord. Alleluja!

This piece is far more subjective than the Palestrina composition, for it is written in such a way that the attention of the listener is directed both to the expressiveness of the music and the words. If proof is needed for this conclusion, we see in the score an extravagant use of chromatics which give to the music an unusual harmonic color. Also, in several sections of the music all of the voices move together and sing each syllable and each word at the same moment. *Homophony* is the musical term for this process, and when it is contrasted with the polyphonic portions of the score the music is more interesting to sing and hear. Because the piece is both expressive and subjective, within the limits of good taste the conductor may take some liberties with its interpretation.

[*Performance of* O Magnum Mysterium]

We spoke earlier of the conductor who pays only lip service to style and then devotes most of his energies to the development of choral tone. Let us suppose that he is one who considers *blend* to be the most important element in the sound of his choir. The technical part of his rehearsal will proceed something like this: (1) Use "oo" vowel with girls—soft singing. (2) Match voices—one section only. (3) Head voice for men—employ descending scales. (4) Sing a short section of the *Sanctus*. This tone and the sacred music of the Renaissance period are beautifully matched. If we desire a tone which is even more impersonal, we can ask the women to sing without any vibrato and this, then, is the result.

[*Chorus sings without vibrato.*]

For our purposes let us classify this kind of sound as "Tone A." If a choir has been drilled to produce this sound over a long period of time, every gesture and movement of the conductor, his facial expression and his instructions will have been coordinated to gain the desired result. Now, let us suppose that he presents to his chorus a piece of music written during the 19th century. Broadly speaking, this music demands of the ensemble the ability to sing with rhythmic flexibility, varying tone color, contrasting dynamics, that is—loudly and softly—and above all with energetic vitality.

[*Performance of* Gloria *with "Tone A"*]

It is obvious that "Tone A" does not meet the requirements of this selection from the Russian liturgy. It is sweet and aesthetically acceptable, but stylistically leaves much to be desired. The tone forces us to listen to *sounds* rather than to a literal interpretation of the text, and the latter is the first and most important requirement in the performance of 19th century music. We will take now a very few minutes to build a tone according to the desire of a conductor who enjoys hearing from his choirs a big tone; full, dark, vital, intense. Perhaps this is the way that he will set about achieving it: (1) Dark "ay" for girls—driving attack, jaws down, etc. (2) Dark "oo" for men. (3) Shout for men— "What shall I say," etc. (4) Abdominal breathing; use four vowel sounds. (5) Sing selected sections of the *Gloria*.

While many choirs in the middle west use "Tone A" for their singing, you will hear "Tone B," the full throated, vital kind of sound, throughout Texas and the south. If time were available we might demonstrate "Tone C" which is based upon the three instrumental sections of an orchestra: string, woodwinds, and brass. No percussion, of course! Then, there is "Tone D" which takes its approach from the phonetics involved in the sounds of vowels and consonants. "Tone E" is developed directly from the rhythmic groupings in any musical score.

For our purposes let us classify this kind of sound as "Tone A." If a choir has been drilled to produce this sound over a long period of time, every gesture and movement of the conductor, his facial expression, and his instructions will have been coordinated to gain the desired result.

All of these methods or systems have merit. Each develops a basic tone which is effective in singing some but not all kinds of music. The question naturally arises, Can the singer change his vocal production and his interpretive ideas to suit every new composition? Some conductors believe that this is possible; I do not agree. Our greatest operatic singers are specialists. They are not adept with all roles, and very few can present an acceptable song recital. The chorus is under a far greater handicap in this respect than is the soloist, for in front of them stands one who is almost powerless to change the way that he responds to music. The strength of his beat, the nature of attack and release, the duration of vowel and consonant sounds, his response to rhythm, to dynamics, to balance and to every other factor involved with singing is the musical extension of his imagination and his personality. He cannot *will* himself to change from song to song, and neither can his chorus.

From the discussion and demonstrations this evening, we come to these conclusions:

First, a continuing choral tradition is possible only when the conductor draws upon both his musical scholarship *and* his understanding of technique. There is a close relationship between the problem of tonal development and the structure of a musical composition. If either factor is considered unimportant, performances will be hackneyed, inartistic and lacking in integrity.

Second, a conductor cannot change materially the sound of his chorus. In reality, he has no wish to do so.

Third, if we accept the premise that the basic sound of a chorus shows little change regardless of what is sung, it follows that the choir cannot perform all music equally well. It is most effective in singing music which in style and structure is best suited to the tone of the group.

Fourth, if a conductor emphasizes unduly one interpretive technique, he may do so at the expense of another. For example—he cannot have both a perfect blend and a magnificent fortissimo from his chorus.

Fifth, perhaps it is superfluous to remind ourselves that popularity and artistry are not necessarily found in the same place.

May I now express our thanks to the members of the Glee Clubs and to James Livengood for their presence here this evening. They know the necessity for the long hours of hard rehearsal which is a basic requirement for beautiful singing. Their attitude and that of every serious musician is exemplified in the words of F. Melius Christiansen which were spoken in Los Angeles many years ago. Dr. Christiansen was the founder and conductor of the first great college chorus in America, the St. Olaf Choir of Northfield, Minnesota. Although he disliked speaking in public, he had been persuaded to come to Los Angeles to tell us of his methods, those techniques which made his choir such a magnificent choral instrument. The occasion was a luncheon meeting, and the place was filled to capacity. Finally, the auspicious moment arrived. Dr. Christiansen rose to his feet, ran his hands through a mass of white hair, and began to speak: "So I am supposed to tell you vat ve do at St. Olaf's to sing vell, to sing mit beauty. Vell, ve yust vurk and vurk and vurk." Then he sat down. And that is what I am about to do.

The Interpretation and Performance of Classical and Romantic Choral Music — A Practical Approach

In a lecture delivered to the October 1970 institute of the Southern California Vocal Association, Swan focuses on the expectations inherent in the stylistic interpretation of Haydn, Mozart, Brahms, and other composers, recounting the necessity for the scholarship demanded of all conductors.

I'm sure you understand that when you attend a university, or when you study with an eminent scholar like Julius Herford, you work for a semester on the music of one man: Mozart or Bach. And then one just makes a beginning. So here we are, in approximately an hour and a half this morning, hoping to learn all that there is to know about the interpretation of two periods of composition. I seem to say this facetiously. Yet, I always have a gnawing fear that because teachers are as they are (and I would remind you that I am a teacher, too), they have to save time. With five or six class assignments and the extra kinds of things we are asked to do, we are always looking for ways to cut corners. Therefore, if we can find out how to do something in ten easy lessons, or failing that, are able to put something down, one-two-three-four-five-six-seven, we do it. But, ladies and gentlemen, if we are going to be interpreters we cannot avoid scholarship. Maybe you don't like that word. Perhaps you don't like the term "academic." Maybe you don't like to read. But if you don't, there isn't any easy way to do this job. One has to engage in some study. All I can do this morning is suggest some ways you can carry on and accomplish much.

This business of style involves three or four commitments on our part. In the first place, we must accept the premise that we are willing to see the composition through the eyes of the composer. Whether we are interested in choral sound, or choral interpretation, or choral performance, or rhythm, or phrasing, or whatever—basically, one accepts the premise that if there is to be a proper style and interpretation,

If we are going to be interpreters we cannot avoid scholarship. Maybe you don't like that word. Perhaps you don't like the term "academic." Maybe you don't like to read. But if you don't, there isn't any easy way to this job. One has to engage in some study.

the compositions must sound as the composer heard them. It is not going to be your composition; it is going to be theirs. This principle varies with the several stylistic periods, but we have to make this kind of commitment to any composer. Then we must make a promise to ourselves even though we know we can never achieve a complete authenticity of interpretation. If my choir, here in this chapel, sings a Bach motet, this chapel is not St. Thomaskirke in Leipzig. These are not the same times in which Bach lived. We will not be using his same instruments for accompaniment. But, you will try to get as close to the meaning and style of the score as is possible though you know you can never achieve a completely authentic performance. This is the second act of commitment which we make as we attempt to build an acceptable interpretation for the presentation of any composition.

In the third place, if we are really interested in stylistic interpretation, we must learn about the times which produced the composer and his works. How did people live and think and act and dress? How concerned were they with music? To what instruments did they listen? What was their sound? Because of their environment, which to some extent shaped their ideas, all composers who lived in a certain period wrote compositions which would be somewhat alike in their construction and sound. That is why we speak of "music of the Classic Period," "music of the Renaissance," etc. There are some features about the music, regardless of the composer, which will be representative of each period. Mozart and Haydn, to some degree, wrote alike. Therefore, there are stylistic rules, factors, techniques which relate to each period of composition. But the sad fact, my friends, is that this is where most conductors stop. They memorize the stylistic factors for a particular period and this is the limit of what they do to achieve proper interpretation.

Yet, there are obvious factors that distinguish the writings of one composer from another. Bach didn't write altogether like Handel. We know that Victoria didn't write like Palestrina. We know that Mozart didn't write like Haydn. We know that. What I am saying is that there are factors in addition to the stylistic factors which relate to the *period*. Yet even this does not go far enough for a proper study. Sometimes, composers wrote differently in one period than they did at another time in their lives. Bach did not compose in exactly the same manner throughout his life. Neither did Mozart. At one point in his career Mozart was employed by the Archbishop of Salzburg who directed him that he produce masses that would not take more than forty-five minutes to sing. As the Archbishop told him, "I do not propose to dance on one foot at the altar while your choir is singing away. So make it brief." Thus, while Mozart cordially hated the Archbishop we can thank him for those beautiful *Missa Brevises* which Mozart left to us. But when we compare the music of the *Missa Brevises* with the scores

Music has not failed us, it is we who at times fail music. We have depended upon gadgets and gimmicks, methods and procedures— many of which are outdated—to make our music successful. And all the while our principal purpose should be that of allowing music to speak for itself.—**"Symposium Summary, Observations and Reflections,"** *Southwestern Musician*, **December 1977.**

of the Mozart *Requiem* or the great *Mass in C minor*, or *Don Giovanni*, or *The Magic Flute*, or the Masonic music, is each the same? Of course not. Haydn had one compositional period when storm and stress were prominent. Yet, when these scores are compared with his early masses, the later masses, and finally, the *Creation*, we find this oratorio to be exceedingly romantic in style and structure. What I'm saying is this: it isn't enough simply to know the composer and say, "Ah yes, Mozart wrote this way, or this is appropriate to Mozart." That is not enough; we have to go further. We have to recognize that one composition of each composer is going to be different from another composition by the same composer. We have to learn to read the score and understand its sound. One cannot say that the Brahms *Requiem* sounds exactly like the *Liebeslieder waltzes*. But they were both written by Brahms, and both compositions carry the stamp of his genius.

With these premises in mind, let us look at the period we call "Classical." Donald Grout says four aspects of the eighteenth-century life and thought are especially important for our understanding of this period. In the first place, the Classical Period was a cosmopolitan age

Conducting the "Stairway to the Stars" festival for the Santa Monica (California) City Schools

85

"which desired a music composed of the best features contributed by all nations." This is important. The music was not regional or nationalistic. For the first time, music took on attributes of the *universal*. Grout says in the second place: "This was a humanitarian age." Not that we would know it as such today. But speaking historically, this was an age of enlightened despots. Thirdly, "This [the Classical Period] was an age for the popularization of art." Composers began to take notice of a general public for music. Do we all recognize, for example, that Haydn was the last great composer who had a patron? Doesn't that make a difference to you and your audience? Do you ever think in terms of the audience as you prepare your works? I think you do. Would it have made a difference in a composer's writing if he were forced to think of where his next loaf of bread was coming from? Would this make any difference in our interpretation of his works? I think so! Finally, Grout speaks of this period as a prosaic age. You lovers of the Baroque, listen to this: "This age [the Classical Period] had little liking for Baroque mysticism, gravity, massiveness, grandeur and passion."[1] The task of these people was to imitate nature. Not to tell it like it was, but to tell it like they imagined it to be; to offer to the listener pleasant sounding images of reality.

The great historian, Dr. Burney, wrote: "Music was a decorative art and an innocent luxury."[2] Music should never compel the listener to understand what was going on. "It should astonish by elaborate excessive elaboration, or ever puzzle by too great complexity. The ideal music should be noble as well as entertaining. Not limited by national boundaries, it should be expressive within the bounds of decorum."[3]

Let me stop here. When you conduct your Mozart, even the Mozart *Requiem*, does what you do dynamically or with the tone or with the tempo startle people? There are two or three places where Mozart expects his music to surprise. What does he do to achieve such a result? He notates these dynamic changes, even in *that* early period! *Subito piano* and *subito forte*; these are typical Mozartian expression marks. It is almost as though he is saying, "let this music unfold, don't do things to it." Unfortunately, what do we hear in many of the performances of the *Requiem*? In the *Tuba Mirum*, for example, the bass soloist takes great liberties with the dynamics and with phrasing and makes the piece blatantly romantic. What do many conductors say when they arrive at the *Dies Irae*? They rub their hands together with glee and say, "It is time to show them the flames!" Their *Requiem* be-

---

[1] Donald J. Grout, *A History of Western Music*, (New York: W.W. Norton, 1960) pp. 412-414.
[2] Charles Burney, "Essay on Musical Criticism," introducing Book III of his *General History of Music*.
[3] Grout, *Op.Cit.* pp. 414-415.

comes very exciting in a romantic way. But, this is not style! Remember what was said earlier concerning that which one must promise himself to do if he is to conduct stylistically.

The story of the contemporary interest in matters of style is most interesting. In the early 30's (Yes, I go back that far!), conductors were caught up with the then new and exciting experiences of singing music "a cappella." Thus, most of the time before the advent of World War II was used in the exploration of choral techniques. How should we rehearse when the choir was to sing "a cappella?" In the years following the conclusion of the war, we became concerned with the development of choral tone; we talked about and experimented with techniques having to do with choral blend and balance. Because of the exciting results achieved by a young man named Robert Shaw, there were many who became convinced that the greatest single factor in choral performance had to be rhythmic vitality. If you could secure the right sort of bounce, you really had an outstanding choir!

How have matters changed in the past ten years? We now talk of style and interpretation and performance practices. This is now the "fashionable" thing. Every time one attends a conference one hears discussions and sees demonstrations concerned with stylistic characteristics. Style—the perception of what is right and what is wrong in interpreting music—is learned *both* with the heart and with the head. With the "heart" we admire the composer and the music. With the "mind" we understand what is taking place in the score. Unless we use both heart and mind, the ideas of the composer cannot be presented authentically, and we do a great disservice to our choirs, to the composer, and to ourselves.

Let us characterize this period in music terms. How is the music of the Classical Period different from that composed at other times? Are you interested in tone? Most of the choral tone to be used in performing the music of this period is both bright and small in sound. What about pulsation? Such should be light and delicate and very precise. It should sound as though we are conducting with only the fingers; no drive of the arm or shoulder is effective. Constantly ask yourself this question as you conduct music of this period: "Does my beat change? Do I 'change' as I direct Palestrina, Bach, Brahms, and then Mozart? Or, do I present myself to my choirs in exactly the same fashion—regardless of period or composer of score?" Tempos of the music of the Classical Period change very little during the performance of a composition. When there is a change, such takes place with the beginning of a new section. When there is a new musical or textual idea, there will be little or no use of rubato. Melody is supreme. There is comparatively little contrapuntal writing; when such appears it is usually developed from a harmonic basis. There continues to be much use of ornamentation. How much do we know of ornaments? Are we afraid

Style—the perception of what is right and what is wrong in interpreting music—is learned both *with the heart and with the head. With the "heart" we admire the composer and the music. With the "mind" we understand what is taking place in the score.*

to use them? Why don't we create our own as did the performers of the time? "But," you say, "How do I start?" Begin with Robert Donington's article on "ornamentation" in Grove's Dictionary. Go on from this study to a much more precise and detailed exploration in his book, *The Interpretation of Early Music*. Read the excellent statements in the books authored by Arnold Dolmetsch and Thurston Dart.[4] If Mozart is performed without the use of any embellishment or by inserting and using the wrong ones—how then can we claim to know proper style and performance practice?

Perhaps the most important stylistic fact about the music of this period is this: Nothing which we do interpretively should disturb the structure or the form of the composition. The structure of a piece of music is almost more important than its content, for that is the way these composers thought of their own scores.

The two giants of the Classical Period obviously are Mozart and Haydn. What is the basic difference in their music? With Haydn we seek interpretively for *rhythmic* consideration, and in Mozart's compositions we must be sensitive to the demands of *melody*. In the June, 1960 Bulletin of the American Choral Foundation there is an article titled, "General Considerations in Performing Haydn and Mozart" written by Jan LaRue. There it all is: 1, 2, 3, 4, 5, 6, 7, etc. It tells when and why organ should be used instead of harpsichord. It tells us what has happened to the figured bass of the Baroque Period. It advocates the use of smaller choruses to sing the music of this period and all this implies with respect to interpretation. You will find it to be a most helpful reference.

Let us now turn our attention to Mozart's *Solemn Vespers K339*. Mozart shows himself to be both daring and innovative in the writing of this piece. See what he does with his choice of keys. The first movement—the *Dixit*—is in C Major. The second movement, the *Confiteor*, in E♭ Major; the *Beatus Vir*, G Major; the *Laudate Pueri*, in D Minor; the *Laudate Dominum* in F Major; and the *Magnificat* in C Major. To use such varied keys was not at all habitual for the composers of this period. Why, then, does Mozart use such a technique? I think that he wants *color*. He uses the same device in many of his operas and with his setting of the *Requiem*. The most unusual thing about the fugue (*Laudite Pueri*) is the leap downward of the diminished seventh. See what the bass does in the fourth measure followed by the tenors in their fourth measure. This is a reminder of Handel's *Messiah* and its use goes all the way back to Pachalbel. Why the diminished seventh? Because Mozart thought about it on one dark night? No—*color*; a kind of harmonic and rhythmic bite that such gives to a composition. In this piece, the singers should think in terms of dancing, or in terms

Every successful choral conductor must function effectively in several roles. He is an <u>organizer</u> of time and activity, a <u>technician</u> as he works with the tonal and musical resources of his choir, a <u>communicator</u> of musical ideas to performer and auditor, a <u>listener</u> to all kinds of live and recorded performance, an <u>educator</u> as he attempts to make those about him understand and appreciate musical values, a <u>scholar</u> and an <u>interpreter</u> of that which is found in the score.—"Guest Editorial," *The Choral Journal*, **March 1972.**

---

[4] Thurston Dart, *The Interpretation of Music*, (New York: Harper and Row. 1953).

of playing in the upper part of the piano with the little finger of the right hand. Think in terms of a string quartet playing by candlelight, perhaps in the Mirabell Palace in Salzburg. If we allow our singers to go "on their own" we may have the notes of Mozart, but the style of the Verdi *Requiem*. We must train them to sing with the right kind of energy: light, controlled, and flexible. Furthermore, the conductor much change and adjust the conducting beat to suit the style of the music. With the music of the Classical Period we must change our ideas of intensity, both in the way we conduct and how we ask our singers to sing. We even have to change ideas as we move from one movement to another in the same score. Isn't rhythm and precision more important in the *Laudate Pueri,* and isn't melody more important in the *Laudate Dominum*? We have to change, but, we must remember that all of it is Mozart. Our interpretation must be the application in sound of Classical principles.

Let us look now at the music of the Romantic Period. First, I would like to discuss several beliefs which have influenced choral conductors for such a long time that they are considered by some to be almost as sacred as the Ten Commandments. The first principle that satisfies many of us (and we don't need the other nine) is stated in this fashion: "Oh, it is easy to conduct Romantic music—you just be yourself," or "This music is so subjective that one may interpret it according to individual emotion and musical taste." However, those who know a great deal more than we, do not believe that the interpretation of Romantic music is such an easy task. Alfred Einstein, whom I admire very much for a number of books which he has authored, says that the first facts that we should remember are the *great contrasts* in the music of the period. First, there is the contrast of the theatrical with the intimate. Secondly, we will find differences between the subjective and the objective. Third, there is the contrast of clarity and a profound mystical quality. Think, on the one hand, of the music of Mendelssohn as compared with that of Berlioz. Can we interpret their music in exactly the same terms? The fourth contrast, says Einstein, is that of absolute and program music.[5] He says that "we are indebted to Mendelssohn for the finest statement ever made in justification of absolute music: in a letter of October 15, 1842, he said that the thoughts which good compositions express are not too vague to be contained in words but too definite. Good music, he says, does not become more significant or intelligible through 'poetic' interpretations; instead it becomes less significant, less clear."[6]

What about many choral conductors' Romantic interpretations? Are we doing just the opposite of what we think we are doing, by

What about many choral conductors' Romantic interpretations? Are we doing just the opposite of what we think we are doing, by smearing certain Romantic compositions with sudden changes in tempi, dynamics, and phrasing, or inordinate involvement with rubato?

---

[5] Alfred Einstein, *Music in the Romantic Era*, (New York: W.W. Norton, 1947) pp. 4-7.

[6] Einstein, *Op. Cit*. p. 6.

smearing certain Romantic compositions with sudden changes in tempi, dynamics, and phrasing, or inordinate involvement with rubato?

There are some unifying principles in Romantic music, says Einstein. First and foremost, we must remember the preoccupation of the times with new sounds for voice and instrument. No matter which Romantic composer you are thinking of whether Brahms or Wagner, Mendelssohn or Berlioz, all had a preoccupation with different sounds and colors. There were many ways of achieving exciting objectives, whether such was in the area of the harmonic, the rhythmic or the dynamic elements of music. Apropos of this kind of activity Einstein makes this clever statement: "The only thing that a Romantic is unable to write is abstract music."[7]

For the first time in history the Romantic composers wrote for a public which they did not expect to see and know. The Romantic composers wrote for eternity. For whom did Haydn write? For the Esterhazys; for the musical public in Vienna and London. For whom did Mozart write? For whom did Bach write? For their patrons and employers. But the Romantic wrote with the belief that his was the music that would last forever. He wrote for a public which he needed, but in many cases which he despised at the same time he was accepting its adulation.

Nineteenth-century music *was* different. Now, there was a national music. There was an interest in folk music. There was an interest in words, in ideas, in poetry. This thought of Einstein's is interesting. He says: "Music is not in all periods the direct expression of the spirit in that particular century. . . . Many periods create for themselves the music that they need." The nineteenth century was the century in which the great revolutions were born that eventually left behind the economic and political upheaval of the Napoleonic Wars. Einstein goes on to say, "Since 1815, in practically all of Europe things had been peaceful. Therefore, romantic music in part was created because people wanted to be stirred up."

What of the Romantic spirit as expressed in music terms? Color was now cultivated for itself: harmonically, rhythmically, and dynamically. Cadences were avoided and resolved deceptively. What about musical phrases? Do we find the short phrases of the Classical Period? Not at all. Now they are both long and short, and arrived at unexpectedly. As the mood changes, so does the tempo. Not always are changes made at sectional points. There is no use of proportional tempos; rather we find the extremes in tempos, extremes in dynamics and a great use of tempo rubato. All of this because the people of the times

---

[7] Einstein, *Op. Cit.* p. 8.

were entranced with color. Harmony now is more important than counterpoint. Expressiveness is linked to the meaning of words.[8]

What about the conducting of Romantic music? In some ways, Romantic music is the most difficult for the average person to conduct. This is so because one cannot, will not, or does not believe in a legitimate response to the imaginative demands of the score. Unfortunately, this conductor refuses to become a creative, imaginative kind of person. Yet, one cannot be a well-organized, cool, psychologically complete, objective personality and conduct successfully Romantic music. May I say it even more strongly? We cannot direct Romantic music and be the least bit self-conscious about ourselves. This is the test. Are you willing to quote poetry to your chorus? Which means, of course, that you have read it and you can respond to its message. One doesn't know intuitively what beauty is in this world; one has to *learn* how to appreciate it. Many of us are not willing to take the time for that sort of preparation.

I sat here this morning for thirty minutes as you came into this chapel. There are four very different and magnificent windows in this room. Yet, not one person came up to look at the detail in the windows. This is the way we are so often. We are too busy for beauty. And yet, you wish to take this music that was the expression of a musical poet and interpret it.

What can we do to help with our interpretation of these scores? We must learn to talk with metaphors. We must know how to use analogy. How in the world will we talk in analogy if we have had no experiences which involve beauty? We cannot rehearse constantly in terms of: "Now, listen for this. Now, blend here. Now, do this rhythmically. Now, phrase here like this." Such rehearsal techniques do not furnish all of the answers for Romantic music. So, for many of us, Romantic music is not worth the effort. We are too busy. We have papers to read. We have reports to fill out.

Because of the emphasis upon the individual singer during this period (lieder, oratorio, opera, etc.) we have responsibilities as we conduct and interpret Romantic music. What do we know about choral tone if in this period as in no other the singer's instrument is so very important? Voices must be allowed to operate freely and imaginatively and with proper vocal technique. Can we teach people how to interpret with their voices? How much do we know about building the vocal instrument? These are some of the many questions we ask about the sound of Romantic music.

It is rather obvious that in the few minutes we have left, we cannot talk about Mendelssohn and Schubert and Berlioz and Bruckner and Mahler and Brahms and Vaughan Williams and the other composers

_____
[8] Einstein, *Op. Cit.* pp. 21-24.

Learning how to listen means "what can you turn off?" so you can devote all of your abilities to concentrate on matters which are most important to hear at a given moment.

of the Romantic song. We are going to listen to Mr. Ben Bollinger's Chamber Chorale from Citrus College as they sing two very beautiful Romantic pieces: one composed by Verdi, and the other by Brahms. For what will you in the audience listen? Turn on your ears. Don't listen to this chorus in terms of the usual choral techniques. We are dealing with style this morning. With how much color does this choir sing? Why? What is there in the composition which makes the chorus sing in a special way? I think you'll find that in the Verdi, color in sound is made by the intervals and the chromatics which Verdi employs. I think you'll find in the Brahms that the color is made by the quality of sound in the lower voices. What kind of production and phrasing characterizes the singing of the choir? You people who have been in my classes know that we make quite a thing out of learning how to listen. Learning how to listen means "what can you turn off" so you can devote all of your abilities to concentrate on matters which are most important to hear at a given moment. If you learn how to do this, the next time you hear the Roger Wagner Chorale or any other chorus presenting a great concert you will enjoy a magnificent experience. "Press the red button" and listen. Then, "press the blue button" and listen to something else. Once again, "press the yellow button" and listen to still another technique or attribute. Press all three of them and have a lot of fun for yourself. It is just like playing a chord organ!

(*Chorale sings : "Im Herbst" by Brahms and "Ave Maria" by Verdi.*)

In the Verdi composition, if we understand and teach techniques by which the voice is made free for proper expressions we are confronted with a conflict. We cannot allow an interpretive freedom vocally for each singer because the chorus may lose control over one important factor in the score; namely, a proper concern for intervals. This is especially true when Verdi uses so many accidentals in his compositions. This is one great danger in the rendition of Romantic music. If one becomes too subjective both conductor and singers lose control. Have you ever had this experience after a concert? You are on "cloud nine!" You confer with a friend and say, "Wasn't that wonderful? Didn't the choir sing magnificently?" Then, the person replies: "Well, I didn't hear anything particularly different from your other performances! As a matter of fact, I thought it was a little sloppy in spots!"

Here is an interesting fact concerning "Im Herbst." Geiringer tells us that originally this piece (#4 of Op. 104) was composed a third lower because Brahms wanted it to sound especially dark and somber. All five of the works in Op. 104 are extremely dark in color, and Brahms wanted this one to be even darker than any of the others in the set. After his first sketches, however, he realized that the altos and basses would have be having so much trouble with the tessitura in which he was asking them to sing that he transposed it up a third. This

---

Perhaps those of us who have responsibilities for the teaching of music or for some other form of musical activity to some degree have forgotten what music is. So often we confuse methods and procedures with music's substance—its reason for being. Music is aesthetic. It appeals to people because it possesses elements of beauty, expressed both in form and sound. It cannot be defined in scientific terms, yet this is a virtue rather than a hindrance, for the ambiguous, indefinable character makes it an art that is important to different people for different reasons. Though we all know this, I wonder if we haven't tried to build an army of music lovers who we expect automatically and uniformly to respond to our own particular goals and objectives.— **"Symposium Summary, Observations and Reflections,"** *Southwestern Musician,* **December 1977.**

is an indication of the "darkness" that Brahms desired to be heard in this piece.

Because there is such a wonderful combination of the Classical and the Romantic in the compositions of Beethoven, the Chorale will sing the *Hallelujah* from the *Mount of Olives*. How many of the Classical interpretive characteristics will you hear? You are going to hear some Handel in this piece; Haydn is also represented and you will also hear some "Romantic" musical ideas.

A very helpful series of articles in the *Music Educators Journal*, titled "Singing in Style," was authored some time ago by Edward Mennerth. These began with the summer 1966 issue and carried forward with a discussion of all the periods of musical composition. Mennerth writes with great authority; study what he has to say.

I want to thank this wonderful group of young people and their conductor, Mr. Bollinger. I want to thank you, the audience, for coming, not only because I have many friends in front of me, but because when you come in such numbers you encourage anyone who wonders about the state of music these days. Surely music is doing something right when a group of 200 music educators comes out on a Saturday morning. Don't give your music making a half-hearted kind of service. This art deserves the service of both mind and heart. Such is the only way to learn how to interpret the music of the masters.

Three "T's" for Choral Success

In this paper, Swan provides the reader with his insightful account of the "three important areas of investigation and practice contributing to musical success" — tone, technique, and tradition.

1. Tone

There are many ways to study a musical score and make it come alive in sound and interpretation. However, all who conduct choral groups regardless of the age or proficiency of their singers should be concerned with three important areas of investigation and practice which will help in contributing to a successful musical experience. One might term these the three "T's": Tone—Technique—Tradition (style). In every musical score these three elements possess a different degree of relevance or importance; they also are related in many ways and one must learn how to rehearse to solve the problemls prompted by the three "T's."

What can be said concerning the first "T"? Are there common procedures which can be utilized for the process of building an acceptable choral sound? Because quality of tone to some degree is shaped by physical, mental, and emotional factors in addition to obvious vocal skills—are choral conductors prepared to make decisions concerning the sound which they wish to hear eventually from their singers? I believe that this sound will reflect the conductor's acceptance of principles concerning: 1) The relative importance of specific choral techniques such as blend, balance, precision, rhythmic vitality, etc.; 2) the relationship of tone to matters of style and performance practice; 3) the nature of the repertoire favored by the conductor. When one considers the influence exerted by these several factors together with individual verbal and physical singularities which appear in the moods and actions of every director, it is easily understood why no two choruses in America are alike in their sound. Nor will their conductors agree as to the nature and aesthetic of a satisfying and beautiful tone quality.

Since the choice of a pleasing choral sound is a matter for individual decision, I present my principles and procedures without apology. This is the way "I would do it"; others may prefer measures which are quite different from my own.

I begin with the conviction that we must know our singers as persons before we can help to build their voices. Whether in a church, school or community situation, a director should plan to listen to the choristers individually at least once during each choral season. Depending upon the age and experience of the group, this might be the way an interview or audition could proceed:

(1). *Evaluation of Speech*—rate, pitch, resonance, content. I am anxious to learn something of the imaginative qualities possessed by each individual. Thus, at one point (for those new to me) I ask, "Do you like to sing?" "Why?" The answers are quite revealing!

(2). *An Appraisal of Posture*—including stance, jaw, throat, mouth.

(3). *Musicianship*—(obviously, a junior choir member will not be tested in the same way as an older or experienced person). Basically, I am anxious to ascertain the ability of the singer to hear, to respond properly to *rhythmic* patterns, and in advanced musical situations *to read at sight*. Frequent use is made of Louis Diercks' tonal memory prognostic test which is an excellent guide to intervallic and rhythmic skills and also may be used to screen large groups of singers.[1]

(4). *Evaluation of Voice*—range, quality, registration. Whether one uses the terms "warmup" or "vocalization" I would hope for agreement as to the importance of vocal and physical exercise in building voices. Also, there are some procedures which, if they receive constant use, can lead to anticipated results. For example: (a) The *direction* of the vocalise will strengthen either the lower or the upper registration in the voice. Too many exercises always begin low and move high, and this effectively hinders the growth of the "head" of passagio registration. (b) A *continuous* use either of legato or marcato exercises will affect adversely the phonation of the singers, the development of a rhythmic vitality, and the ability to recognize and use the several dynamic levels. (c) A *constant* use either of soft or loud singing in time will make it impossible for the vocalist to respect the wishes of a composer concerning dynamic changes and the use of crescendo and diminuendo. (d) An overindulgence in vocalizing with any single vowel or syllable will bring results which may be those desired by an experienced teacher but will be disappointing to one who is not yet acquainted with voices. There are differences in "open" and "closed"

[1] Louis H. Diercks, "A Progressive Approach to the Choral Audition," *The Choral Journal*, (November 1972), p. 9.

Tonal Memory Test

Instructions for administering this Tonal Memory Test:

Tell the singer that each of the 7 short melodic figures will be played *only once*. After each figure is played, the singer is to sing it back on the sylable "LA". Both the pitches and the rhythm are to be sung correctly.

For the auditioner to count the figure as correct, *all* pitched and rhythms must be accurate.

MM: ♩ = 76

97

vowel sounds, in consonants which either are exploded or carry pitch. The English "ay" and "o" are dipthongs, and there are differences in placement for "oo," "ah," and "ee." The wise teacher will vary vocalizations and will learn to select such with care if a particular result is desired.

An outline for the initial development of tone in a chorus might be something like this:

(1) Discovery of the basic vocal potential of each singer with an audition or conference.

(2) The correction of posture including stance—jaw, mouth, and lips.

(3) The building of support for the tone—use of breath, phonation, etc.

(4) The establishment of an authentic and uniform pronunciation and articulation.

(5) The extension of range for each singer.

It is almost a certainty that as choral directors learn to know their singers better, special vocal problems will become evident. These may include: breathiness in the tone, a nasal tone production, tremolo versus a normal vibrato, and the necessity to modify vowel sounds. However, positive results might be heard in the development of a full bodied tone, the extension of range, and the establishment of registers in each voice.

In this short presentation, it is not possible to suggest exercises which will aid in solving all or specific vocal problems. A brief bibliography which can help in this regard may be found at the close of this paper. However, one should remember that as knowledge concerning the singing process grows, so also will the desire for a particular choral sound and a method or practice to achieve it. Regardless of problems, satisfaction will come when a choral ensemble produces a tone which aesthetically is beautiful—which is achieved with no harm done to the voices of the singers and which serves effectively a considerable number of compositions representing many styles and periods.

2. Technique

A vocabulary of musical terms does not have the same meanings for all who are associated with the profession. Witness "tremolo." In instrumental circles its use is considered to be both important and necessary. On the other hand, for singers and their teachers, the same work is descriptive of a dismal sound which results from poor vocal production, a lack of proper physical support for the tone, or perhaps comes about because of nervous tension on the part of the singer. For the vocal-choral world, "tremolo" is always undesirable; "vibrato" in the tone is considered to be pleasurable to hear and is eagerly sought after by most vocalists.

Another example, the words "balance" or "blend" as used frequently in rehearsals do not have the same meaning for all who teach, sing, or conduct. There is also considerable difficulty with the development of a common understanding for such words as "phrasing," "nuance," "intensity," and other similar expressions.

So it is with the word "technique." A perusal of contemporary texts finds in one volume this term used to describe every activity which takes place in a choral rehearsal. Another author finds "technique" a suitable word for dealing only with tonal problems. A third definition would limit its use in a choral situation to matters pertaining to communication in the rehearsal or performance.

I prefer to think of choral techniques as the means by which a musical score "comes to life." Some techniques are skills which relate to the process of singing; others basically are mental and are linked to interpretive ideas. Some techniques are unique to choral singing, while others are shared with all who make music, whether such be instance, mental, or vocal and produced by a group or a lone individual. All techniques are named, and thus are nouns; some also are verbs and carry their activity in their nomenclature. Thus, *what* they are is important; *how* and *why* and *when* they operate is essential.

As conductors study a score, they find that its composer requires that certain skills must operate before the piece can communicate and be, in sound, what first had existed only in imagination. These skills become for me my choral technique.

In common with others who have catalogued factors pertaining to the rehearsal of a score, I divide these into five basic groups: tonal, technical, interpretive, stylistic, and formal. (See Figure 2.) Presumably, some tonal and stylistic requirements will be cared for with the use of suggestions made elsewhere in discussing matters relative to "t's" one and three. The following are important techniques needing much rehearsal—how much depends upon the demands of the score. The list includes blend, balance, diction (including textual meaning, sound, and degrees of intensity), intonation, precision of attack and release, use of dynamics, rhythmic sensitivity, and possibly the three most important techniques: tempo choice, phrasing, and musical articulation.

It is wise to make certain preparations before techniques are used in rehearsal. Conductors should define and explain for themselves and for their students the meaning and importance of each technique. Also, the choral director would do well to become familiar with several procedures with which each technique can be rehearsed.

I have found it helpful to fill a notebook with comments concerning the nature and rehearsal of each of the techniques. As an example, I say this about *blend*:

I prefer to think of choral techniques as the means by which a musical score "comes to life."

99

(1). It is not possible to find a definition of the term "blend" in any musical source. However, the dictionary statement is helpful. (To blend is) "to combine or mix so as to render the constituent parts indistinguishable from one another."[2] Musically speaking, the "constituent parts" are the singers in an ensemble. One voice blends into another by establishing a uniform pronunciation, dynamic level and precision of attack and release. This should remain unchanged, regardless of the demands of the score. When a chorus achieves this goal, the aesthetic result is exceedingly beautiful.

(2). Blend is a basic requirement for every chorus. However, the blending of the voices is not easily accomplished when: (a) The ensemble is using a dynamic level higher and stronger than *mf*; (b) The tempo of a piece requires the singers to move rapidly from pitch to pitch; (c) The director asks the choir to sing with great intensity or energy; (d) The score demands of the singers a high degree of subjective thought applied to interpretive principles.

(3). There can be limits to the degree or amount of blend desired by the director. Totality of blend would call for a vibratoless tone.

(4). Blend is enhanced by the precision of attack and release.

(5). Since blend requires uniformity, the classification and seating of the chorus by sections and individually is important. Experiment with placement.

(6). Blend will be achieved only by constant drill—by using a guide which will help to unify pronunciation and by arranging the choir so that all can *hear*.

(7). Blend is important when one is working for an authentic rendition of the older music. Particularly this will be true when the score uses much polyphony.

(8). A chorus which works to perfect blend as a primary goal will not sing as effectively the music of the nineteenth century. Blend then will influence the choice of repertoire.

To practice for blend: much drill—emphasis on listening—rehearsing in circles and changing placement of the choir—talking about pronunciation including pitch, consonants, and dipthongs—making tapes and commenting on the results. However, the most important goal is reserved for the conductor who must make a decision concerning the amount of blend, which for him, is desirable. The choice will be reflected in rehearsals, repertoire, and in performance.

If a conductor attempts to care for *all* of the techniques as shown in the rehearsal plan (Figure 2), he/she will become easily discouraged with the amount of time required for such a task. Fortunately, such is not necessary. The important thing is to ascertain by score study which of the techniques is *essential* for the successful rendition of the piece.

---

[2] *The American Heritage Dictionary of the English Language*.

A folk song must have its melody preserved—a narrative text deserves work on diction—varied phrases are far more important than others where the shape is a constant, etc. In any score there are a half dozen or so of the techniques which must be preserved if the score is to maintain integrity in performance. I like to take a rehearsal plan and indicate on a scale of one to five, those which are the truly important techniques. Then, I begin my rehearsals with these. If time is available, I then reserve practice for other procedures.

At the beginning of this statement, it was said that for each of the three "T's" there was a relevance—a relationship—and the need for rehearsal. The thoughtful conductor will make decisions in each of the three areas knowing that what is done will have its bearing upon all else.

3. Tradition

It is quite impossible to say in a few words all that is important concerning style, tradition, and performance practices. In a limited time all that can be accomplished is to mention some few principles which will serve as guideposts for individual study which may last a lifetime.

One does not conduct music for long without realizing that a score which possesses integrity in its formal aspects and carries possibilities for an artistic interpretation should be somewhat different from all other compositions. A choir may sing with a beautiful tone and can demonstrate remarkable technical skills, but without an understanding of differences in style, every piece in a program will sound alike. Without a proper appreciation for the many approaches to compositional technique, there will be no distinguishing of Bach from Mozart, Victoria from Palestrina, Monteverdi form Gabrieli.

How does a busy conductor learn about style? I believe that the first step is the most difficult. The world-be interpreter must come to a decision concerning the degree of importance to be attached to the principle of *authenticity*. To say it in another way: how much of a composition "belongs" to the composer or to the conductor and choir? Is there any merit in attempting a conclusive performance when it is obviously impossible to recreate the conditions which were responsible for the origin of the piece and the motivation of the composer to write in a particular manner?

Every conductor must decide concerning authenticity. Often its importance varies from one piece to another. There are many reputable musicians who have declared that to carry out this principle is neither possible nor necessary. W. A. Mozart, Leopold Stokowski, and Leonard Bernstein are three who have furnished new *Messiah* instrumen-

One does not conduct music for long without realizing that a score which possesses integrity in its formal aspects and carries possibilities for an artistic interpretation should be somewhat different from all other compositions.

tations to add to Handel's original score. Prominent critics have scoffed at attempts to present Bach's cantatas with the original number of choir boys and baroque instruments together with harpsichord and organ tuned to eighteenth century pitch requirements. These adherents of this subjective and contemporary approach to performance defend their point of view with the assertion:

> If Bach or Palestrina or Mozart were living today and were acquainted with twentieth century instruments and concert halls or the reponse of a modern audience to the nature and length of a program, these three would be composing in a different fashion.

It is perhaps impossible to reproduce today all of the factors which controlled performance in former years. This is particularly true of compositions written in times before scores were printed or perhaps were scarce in number. Many composers were closely involved with the church or the nobility and wrote primarily for their own use. A few brilliant theorists reported from time to time on the state of music, but since a composer did not expect that his pieces would be played or sung in surroundings other than his own, little attention was given to matters of notation or to the practical aspects of performance.

While recognizing the difficulties which accompany contemporary attempts to reproduce the original sounds of instruments and voices, more conductors are determined to do what they can to approximate the wishes of the composer. However, such desires must be accompanied by study, a development of one's ability to hear more and more. Also, and perhaps most importantly, there must be a willingness to compromise and even at times to change concepts and opinions.

Although my proposals might be termed simplistic by scholars who champion the importance of musicological study, I would suggest that one approach to matters of style is to consider the problem as having three dimensions. The first of these and easiest to study, absorb, and learn is the listing of practices which have been relevant to a particular period of composition. Because of geographical, economic, political, social, religious, and musical factors, all composers who lived and worked during a particular period to some degree were alike in their writing.

The periods which are of the most importance to choral musicians are these: Renaissance, Baroque, Classical, Romantic, and Contemporary. In time the serious student-conductor will wish to divide each period into smaller segments for study. Some of these are High and Low Renaissance; the English and the Italian Madrigals; Pre-Classical, including Rococo and Empfindsamer Stil; Impressionism; Avant Garde; and all forms of "Neo" composition; Electronic Media; Twelve Tone Compositions; etc.

The study of compositional techniques which are characteristic of a particular period in music history is a first procedure in learning musical styles. The "second and third steps of the stylistic ladder" are much more difficult and time consuming. At this point it is helpful for the conductor to *compare* composers who worked in the same period: Victoria and Palestrina; Bach and Handel; Mozart and Haydn, etc. In what respects were these men alike in their composing? How different? Why?

Finally, one must study the composition of a single composer. How are these found to be alike and what are the differences among them? Were there periods in the life of the composer when compositional techniques changed? Why? In this regard, think of Handel, Stravinsky, and Schoenberg.

It should be apparent that the writing of scholars who are specialists in the music of a particular period will help greatly as one studies compositional characteristics. Biography, if written free of bias, is of assistance in becoming acquainted with the music masters who were the creative artists of each chronological period. Yet, one needs score study and many listening period with stylistic recordings if interpretations are to be made in good faith.

Here are sample lists of stylistic characteristics for the Renaissance and Baroque periods:

The study of compositional techniques which are characteristic of a particular period in music history is a first procedure in learning musical styles.

Renaissance (High) Sacred Compositional Period

- Music is objective and impersonal
- Dynamics are restricted
- Vibratoless tone (boys' voices)
- Polyphonic settings require work with *imitation* in phrasing, dynamics, pronunciation.
- Tempos basically are steady. Any change in tempo or dynamics is slight and made only when a new section begins.
- Shape of phrase determined by syllabic stress.
- Metrical accents are avoided. No long crescendo.
- From the modal to the tonal. Watch for spots employing musica ficta.
- Textual meaning is not stressed but helps to set the mood.
More important to seasonal motets than in mass settings.

Some additional aids furnished by interview with Hans David and stressed in the volume, *The Art of Polyphonic Song*:

Melody

(1). Notes of equal value that proceed stepwise sing legato.
(2). "Skips" are separated.
(3). The longer the note, the more its intensity.
(4). Short notes are sung lightly.
(5). Notes tied over a bar never should be accented.
(6). Tension should appear in the delivery of an ascending line; relaxation in a descending phrase.

Dynamics

(1). No great contrast in dynamics.
(2). Each phrase has its own dynamic level from which it should deviate only slightly.

(3). The music expresses the mood of the text. However, we must remember that the text is conceived and used according to the meaning, ideas, theology and mores of that period and not as we would think today.[3]

Renaissance Period (Secular Compositions)

Whether one thinks of the Italian or English Madrigal, the French Chanson or the German lieder, the secular music of this period is subjective in sound and text with some use of dynamic change and importance of rhythm and individual tone quality. "Refrains" were common in usage, particularly with the folk compositions.

Baroque Period

(1). Harmony is now chordal. Thus, bass line becomes important which leads to the use of a continuo and in some instances figured bass. Balance is different with soprano and bass lines being predominant in sound.

(2). Instruments are now more important than voices. Harpsichord preeminent.

(3). The people loved color. Color in music was expressed basically through dynamics. Subito changes in dynamics were popular as were "echo" effects. This led to the use and popularity of the concertato device, i.e., the large versus small sounds. Also, this was a time when terraced dynamics were used freely adding or subtracting voices to create larger or smaller sounds.

(4). Expression was determined by the text. Some "emotional outpouring"—universal, not personal.

(5). Unhurried tempos—some use of tempos vibrato—ritard at cadences.

(6). Metrical patterns now used in succession. More pulse.

(7). Individual singers used much ornamentation. At times such also happened to successive choral sections. Very seldom did all of the chorus embellish at the same time.

⟨ Recommended Reading List for Tone ⟩

Ehmann, Wilhelm and Haasemann, Frauke. *Voice Building for Choirs.* Chapel Hill, NC: Hinshaw Music, Inc., 1982.
Heffernan, Charles W. *Choral Music, Technique and Artistry.* Englewood Cliffs, NJ: Prentice-Hall, 1982.

---

[3] Hans T. David. *The ARt of Polyphonic Song* (New York: G. Shirmer, Inc., 1940).

Klein, Joseph J. *Singing Technique*. Princeton, NJ: D. Van Norstrand, 1967.

Miller, Kenneth E. *Principles of Singing*. Englewood Cliffs, NJ: Prentice-Hall, 1983.

Reid, Cornelius L. *The Free Voice*. New York: The Joseph Patelson Music House, 1972.

Robinson, Ray. *Basic Vocal Production*. Chapel Hill, NC: Hinshaw Music, Inc., 1977.

Stanton, Royal. *The Dynamic Choral Conductor*. Delaware Water Gap, PA: Shawnee Press, 1971.

Vernard, William. *Singing, The Mechanism and the Technique*. Los Angeles: University of California, 1964.

⟨ *A Select Bibliography of Books*
Helpful to the Choral Musician
Working With Problems of Tradition and Style ⟩

Abraham, Gerald, ed. *The Age of Humanism, 1540–1630*. London: Oxford University Press, 1968.

Arnold, Denis, and Fortune, Higel, eds. *The Monteverdi Companion*. New York: W. W. Norton, 1972.

Austin, William W. *Music in the Twentieth Century From Debussy Through Stravinsky*. New York: W. W. Norton, 1947.

Bakofzer, Manfred F. *Music in the Baroque Era*. New York: W. W. Norton, 1947.

Dart, Thurston. *The Interpretation of Music*. New York: Harper & Row, 1963.

Dean, Winton. *Handel's Dramatic Oratorios and Masques*. London: Oxford University Press, 1959.

Dolmetsch, Arnold. *The Interpretation of the Music of the XVII and XVIII Centuries Revealed by Contemporary Evidence*. London: Novello, 1946.

Domington, Robert. *Baroque Music, Style and Performance*. New York: W. W. Norton, 1982.

Dorian, Frederick. *The History of Music in Performance: The Art of Musical Interpretation From the Renaissance to Our Day*. New York: W. W. Norton, 1966.

Einstein, Alfred. *The Italian Modrigal*. New Jersey: Princeton University Press, 1949.

Einstein, Alfred. *Music in the Romantic Era*. New York: W. W. Norton, 1947.

Fellowes, Edmund Horace. *The English Madrigal Composers*. London: Oxford University Press, 1948.

Geiringer, Karl. *Haydn: A Creative Life in Music*. Berkeley, CA: University of California Press, 1968.

Geiringer, Karl. *Johann Sebastian Bach: The Culmination of an Era*. New York: Oxford University Press, 1966.

Howerton, George. *Technique and Style in Choral Singing*. New York: Carl Fischer, 1957.

Landon, H. C. Robbins. *Essays on the Viennese Classical Style*. London: Barrie and Rockliff, 1970.

Lang, Paul Henry. *George Frideric Handel*. New York: W. W. Norton, 1966.

LaRue, Jan, ed. *Aspects of Medieval and Renaissance Music: A Birthday Offering to Gustave Reese*. New York: W. W. Norton, 1966.

Mendel, Arthur. "Introduction." *The Passion According to St. John*. J. S. Bach. New York: G. Schirmer, 1951. (Not a book but a classic.)

Moser, Hans J. *Heinrich Schultz; His Life and Work*. Translated by Carl F. Pfatteicher. St. Louis: Concordia, 1959.

Newlin, Dika. *Bruckner, Mahler, Schoenberg*. Morningside Heights, NY: Kings Crown Press, 1947.

Reese, Gustave. *Music in the Renaissance*. New York: W. W. Norton, 1959.

Robinson, Ray and Winold, Allen. *The Choral Experience*. New York: Harper and Row, 1976.

Rosen, Charles. *The Classical Style*. New York: Viking Press, 1971.

Spitta, Philipp. *Johann Sebastian Bach*. London: Novello, 1883. New York: Dover Publications, 1951. (Revised).

Stevens, Denis. *Tudor Church Music*. London: Faber and Faber, 1966.

Strunk, Oliver. *Source Readings in Music History From Classical Antiquity Through the Romantic Era*. New York: W. W. Norton, 1950.

Tovey, Donald Francis. *Essays in Musical Analysis*. Vol. V. *Vocal Music*. London: Oxford University Press, 1956.

Ulrich, Homer. *A Survey of Choral Music*. New York: Harcourt, Brace, Jovanovich, 1973.

Whittacker, W. Gillis. *The Contatas of Johan Sebastian Back*. 2 Vols. London: Oxford University Press, 1959.

Young, Percy M. *The Choral Tradition*. New York: W. W. Norton, 1971.

REHEARSAL PLAN

TITLE _____

COMPOSER _____ Arranger or Editor _____

PUBLISHER _____ Catalog Number _____
FIRST REHEARSAL DATE _____

"WHAT"

TONAL CONSIDERATIONS _____
_____

TECHNICAL FACTORS

Blend   ( ) _____
Balance   ( ) _____
Rhythm   ( ) _____
Attack   ( ) _____
Release   ( ) _____
Diction   ( ) _____
Intonation ( ) _____
Other   ( ) _____

INTERPRETIVE FACTORS

Choice of Tempo   ( ) _____
Phrasing and Nuance   ( ) _____
Dynamics   ( ) _____
Accompaniment   ( ) _____
Other Factors   ( ) _____

STYLISTIC FACTORS

Historical   ( ) _____
Elements of Repetition   ( ) _____
Elements of Contrast   ( ) _____
Elements of Climax   ( ) _____

FORMAL FACTORS

Melodic   ( ) _____
Harmonic   ( ) _____
Rhythmic   ( ) _____
Sectional or ?   ( ) _____

"WHY"—THIS COMPOSITION? (Relative Importance of factors—mood, message, etc.)

_____
_____
_____

IMPORTANT OR UNUSUAL OR DIFFICULT FEATURES ON THE SCORE

_____
_____
_____

THE "HOW AND WHEN" OF REHEARSAL
FIRST REHEARSAL   DATE _____
TIME _____

TO BE PRACTICED   *METHOD*

1. (   ) _____
2. (   ) _____
3. (   ) _____

Summary _____

SECOND REHEARSAL DATE _____
TIME _____

TO BE PRACTICED   *METHOD*

1. (   ) _____
2. (   ) _____
3. (   ) _____
4. (   ) _____

Summary _____

THIRD REHEARSAL DATE _____
TIME _____

TO BE PRACTICED   *METHOD*

1. (   ) _____
2. (   ) _____
3. (   ) _____
4. (   ) _____

Summary _____

4
Credo:
The Choral
Professional

Musical Sounds for the Seventies— Safe, Subversive or Splendid?

With a strong focus on the "art" of communication, Swan addresses the general session of the convention of the Arizona Music Educators Association on the occasion of their 30th anniversary.

This isn't going to be a formal address. Rather, I would like simply to think aloud. I ask that you listen and consider thoughtfully the implications of what I say—not necessarily to agree with my premises and conclusions but hopefully to make some important decisions as to your involvement with music during the next decade.

As the curtain drops on the turbulent sixties, the state of affairs in America and, for that matter, throughout the world is far from encouraging. This is true of all areas of human experience: political, moral, social, economic, cultural. Our changing times breed a spirit of restlessness and suspicion; there exists a vast polarity in opinions expressed on almost any subject. There is disagreement with objective and purpose, and there is conflict and confrontation with those who make the rules and among those who are expected to obey them. Everyone seems to possess the ability and the desire to list problems by the score. Alas, their solution too often is viewed as a wistful hope rather than as accomplished fact. These times bring forth that crowd of pessimists who in the name of what they term "a realistic approach" will say about almost any experience "it won't work"; "there is no solution"; or "I told you that it would end this way."

The musical scene cannot help but reflect these unsettled times. As yet there is no Metropolitan Opera for 1969-70. Some of our most prestigious symphonic organizations are having their problems with administrative procedures, finances, and choice of repertoire. What began several years ago as a bright harbinger for the future—namely, a modest allocation to the arts made by the federal government—now has been all but terminated.

What of school music? In many districts of the country rising costs and a fear of an increase in the tax rate have led to a partial or

111

complete cancellation of music programs by school boards and administrators. Since purposes and objectives of school music are questioned, changed, and sometimes abandoned, teacher training institutions are rightfully confused as they attempt to design a curriculum which will give to prospective teachers the kind of training and knowledge which will enable them eventually to become successful in their profession.

Regents Point Chorale, Christmas 1984

112

Admittedly, all of this makes for a bleak picture. Because things are as they are, it is perhaps easier than ever before for one to be exceedingly pessimistic about the future for music in America and particularly for its stature in our schools. Yet, I would suggest that the immediate future and what it will bring to us and for music, primarily is in our hands. At the risk of being criticized for proposing a capsule solution for the many problems related to music, I would assert that the musical sounds of the seventies will be either safe—or subversive—or splendid. This will depend in large part upon the decisions made by those who teach and perform with school groups. To a considerable degree teachers will determine whether music is to be a powerful artistic and cultural force in society or whether it will become a third rate type of experience endured or ignored by many and nurtured and loved and needed by very few.

There will be those teachers in the seventies who will opt for the "safe" sound. What do I mean by a "safe" music produced by a "safe" teacher? He will be one who always does things in the same way. His procedures, pedagogy, philosophy of music education, terminology, choice of repertoire and lesson plans, will show little change from day to day and year to year. He will view with suspicion anything that is contemporary or new whether this be a Declaration from Tanglewood or the performance of a rock group. If he is a conductor, he will not be able to understand that some music learning must take place in each of his rehearsals—that the emphasis upon performance for its sake alone is not enough. Nor is it valid to hold to the worn-out premise that the principal reason for music's being a part of the school program is because of its invaluable aid in promoting public relations. The "safe" teacher counts the number of concerts which his groups present each year; he is less concerned with their musical standard. This teacher or conductor always has his eye on an opposite number who works at the other end of the city or the state; he must program something which is just as good or better or longer or seemingly more imposing than his competition. He gets by because he keeps on doing his thing, and his thing is the same from year to year. This man doesn't listen to fine recordings or to live performances; he is not aware of the contemporary and exciting shift in objectives for the general music class; he doesn't read; and worst of all, he has stopped thinking.

The dictionary defines the meaning of "subversion" as "the total effect of those actions which cause the utter ruin or destruction of something, or to undermine the allegiance to a faith in something." I submit that by this definition, much so-called music and some who make it are subversive. Those who perform music which is not what it claims to be are subverting the art which they claim to serve. I am not

There is Bach and there is rock, but let us beware when one claims a close relationship with the other. Dishonest music is subversive music. Music making which is subordinated to politics or to society's whims or which masquerades as being "sacred" in character because it is printed in a folio ornamented with lilies and crosses—this is subversive and eventually will destroy the great art which should be protected from such foolishness.

113

now attempting to define that which makes music great or good or simple or complex. There is Bach and there is rock, but let us beware when one claims a close relationship with the other. Dishonest music is subversive music. Music making which is subordinated to politics or to society's whims or which masquerades as being "sacred" in character because it is printed in a folio ornamented with lilies and crosses—this is subversive and eventually will destroy the great art which should be protected from such foolishness. The ironical part of all of this is that we live in the midst of a generation which perhaps as never before is demanding that we tell it as it is, with no subterfuge or apology or cop out. To do anything musical **only** because it is new or different is despicable. Let those of us who claim to be honest in our endeavors look to all of our practices. Do we wax enthusiastic over an exaggerated arrangement of a simple folk song? Do we attempt to make a pops number sound like a tone poem? What about the use of transcriptions? What of those distortions in interpretation which have no foundation in style or proper performance practice—whether such happens as a result of wilful decision or just plain ignorance? I repeat: when there exists in the classroom or the concert hall these examples of a kind of charlatanry—then the cause of music is well on its way to being lost.

Because of its very nature—that which gives it the vitality by which it inspires and changes and makes beautiful the lives of those who come under its spell—because of its special qualities—honest music, sincere music—powerful music—never rings with a hollow sound. It is neither "safe" nor "subversive." Rather it is splendidly satisfying as it has been since the beginning of time. But, in the seventies—such music will demand far more of those who teach and perform. To put it bluntly, those of us who work in the classroom or in the concert hall will be required not only to be fine musicians, with all that this term implies, but also educators, planners, listeners, interpreters, communicators and sincere lovers of everything in this world that is beautiful. And the "everything" includes **people**—who are the most beautiful and wonderful of all things that inhabit this globe.

Do you consider yourself a music educator? Then I would ask this simple question—how much of music in **all** of its aspects do your students learn—appreciate—understand and have affection for as a result of each period of time that they are with you? Do you see a score to some degree through the eyes and ears of your pupils? Do they understand that music is more than mere entertainment or an aesthetic experience? What do your people know of music's history—its form and structure—the elements of time and tone and timbre and dynamics—its harmonies and melodies and rhythms—its stylistic and interpretive aspects? Most important of all—do you plan things so that your students become excited as they find much of this knowledge for them-

114

selves? It is satisfying indeed for a young person in this decade to learn by experience through his science and his mathematics that x + y = z. How much more awesome is the impact which comes with their realization that in all of art, music included, the whole can be more, can be greater than the sum of its related parts!

I've said that the successful teacher of music must be educator, planner, interpreter, listener and communicator. Time does not permit an analysis of each of these areas, but I would like to say something about the teacher as communicator.

Communication and its effective use probably is the most important factor in every phase of contemporary life whether one thinks in terms of political, social or economic phenomena. Relationships among countries, in business, in families—or simply between two individuals succeed or fail as techniques of communication are used successfully or break down partially or completely. As life becomes more complex, we are forced to learn more about the nature of communications. Yet, at the very moment that we are attempting to know more about the subject, its ramifications are growing at such a rate that it is impossible for one person to keep abreast of all that is necessary to know about these admittedly important techniques. You may know that communication has become so specialized that at the higher levels one is forced to approach its data and content by one of three paths: the mathematical, or in terms of language and linguistics, or with the means of behavioral psychology.

I may hasten to say at this point that I know very little about the intricacies of mathematics or linguistics or behavioral psychology. My field is choral music. Yet, there are some simple psychological principles which can be useful to us as we work with students whether this relationship is with an individual or a group.

Let us establish some of these premises and then make their application to varying classroom techniques and situations. First, these axioms from *The Psychology of Communication*, a book written by Jon Eisenson:

> (1) Individuals respond most readily when they are highly involved in the purpose of the communication.
> (2) The psychology of listening equals **attention** and then **perception**.
>> (a) A listener cannot give continuous attention; it comes in spurts.
>> (b) Change is the most basic and significant way to secure attention.
>> (c) Perception (understanding) is achieved through the novelty of the stimulus, through repetition and by the definiteness of **form**.
> (3) The importance of **motivation**.
>> (a) Human beings normally behave in ways that will lead them towards success and achievement.

Those of us who work in the classroom or in the concert hall will be required not only to be fine musicians—with all this term implies—but also educators, planners, listeners, interpreters, communicators and sincere lovers of everything in this world that is beautiful. And the "everything" includes people—who are the most beautiful and wonderful of all things that inhabit this globe.

(b) Human beings like to behave in ways that will help them to gain recognition, admiration, respect and approval.

(c) Human beings generally act in ways that lead towards the realization of a feeling of being wanted.

(d) Human beings seek some adventure—new experiences and zestful living. They tend to avoid boredom and monotony.

Can you begin to see how these axioms are very important if applied properly in a classroom situation or a rehearsal?

Here are some other ideas concerning communication from *The Persuader* by Herbert Abelson. He speaks of the way that opinions and attitudes may be changed:

(1) There will be more opinion change in the desired direction if the communicator has high creditability than if he has low creditability. (He explains that a communicator is seen as credible to the extent that his listeners accept him as first—an expert; second—as trustworthy).

(2) The **motives** attributed to a communicator may affect his success in influencing others.

(3) A communicator's effectiveness is increased if he expresses some views that are also held by his listeners.

(4) The more extreme the opinion change that the communicator asks for, the more actual change he is liable to get.

It is possible to substitute for the term "communicator" the name "teacher" or "performer" or "conductor." Do all of us have "high creditability" with our students? Now—all of us do things in different ways. There is no such thing as a rule book for every teacher to follow. But the successful teachers—the ones who seem to get the most in results from their classes are endowed with these personal traits:

(1) Honesty.

(2) Optimism and the ability to inspire.

(3) Good humor.

(4) Calmness.

(5) Industry.

(6) Courage.

(7) Good taste, appreciation for beauty, an imagination.

(8) A recognition of the worth of the individual.

Now, if all of this sounds corney or preachy or a bit absurd, I'm sorry. As I understand it, however, the good salesman not only is sold on his own product, **he has to know** the individual idiosyncracies of his customers so that he can approach each of them properly and thereby guarantee himself a sale. We know the value of our musical product. Yet, how can we "sell it," that is, convince our classes to give their very best in performance, unless we know each of the students well enough so that like any other salesman we, too, can make an effective approach? Is not this the very essence of communication?

How many times do you think of yourself as belonging to a profession? How many times do you think of yourself with a degree of pride in that you belong to a music profession? This means a next step, namely, we ought to be talking to other people in our profession. . . . Can't you imagine that kind of wonderful feeling that would happen if all who are connected with music worked together on basic problems, not necessarily every day, not necessarily to agree on everything, but when the "chips are down," when music itself was the issue, everybody who knew the power of music, who knew the thrill of music, stood together for the resolution of the problem.—"Symposium Summary, Observations and Reflections," *Southwestern Musician,* December 1977.

May I throw out some questions which I ask myself as I think in terms of communication with my students?

(1) Can I **think** as my young people think? To do this the teacher doesn't have to become a "pal" or one of the gang; they resent this. But a teacher must know the current heroes and heroines of his group and the language with which his students communicate with each other.

(2) Can I convince students that I **need them** to make our shared musical experience effective?

(3) Do I listen—or do I do most of the talking?

(4) Do I know how to **thank** people?

(5) Do I convince my students of my devotion to the music, which in my case, they sing? One does not speak this repeatedly; he does have to **live** it.

(6) Do I always remember that communication procedures change, first with the age, ability, and experience of the class; second with the progress of the class as it proceeds through the school year.

(7) Do I remember that my agencies of communication will change with the nature of the context of that which is taught? What am I stressing in a class or a rehearsal?

(8) Do I know that there are certain ways by which I communicate most effectively, and do I work with these rather than attempting to imitate other communicative techniques used by friends and colleagues?

The art of communication is one means by which a concerned teacher will make his contribution to the sound of music at the present time. If this sound is to be honest and satisfying and splendid, it will be so because he is willing to teach himself much of the technical, the historical, the appreciative and the aesthetic principles which are embodied in every musical score. In my dictionary, the outstanding teacher is never a pessimist, but rather is what I would term an optimistic realist. He is a realist in recognizing his own limitations but is not defeated by them. He is a **realist** in recognizing his own limitations but is not defeated by them. He is a **realist** when he constantly evaluates the abilities of his students. He shows his realism by his constant study; by planning carefully his class presentations and rehearsals; by his experimentation; and by learning to know his people as individuals not just as bodies, names, or numbers.

Yet, he is an optimist, for his faith will never waver in himself, in his students—and most importantly in his music. Because his optimism and his realism are coordinated, he will make it possible for music to speak as clearly and as positively in the seventies as at any time in history.

Safe, subversive, or splendid? What kind of music will we have

The art of communication is one means by which a concerned teacher will make his contribution to the sound of music at the present time. If this sound is to be honest and satisfying and splendid it will be so because he is willing to teach himself much of the technical, the historical, the appreciative and the aesthetic principles which are embodied in every musical score.

in the next ten years? The answer, my friends lies with you and with me.

The Importance of
The Personal Equation

In this article, published in the October 1972 issue of the Choral Journal, *Swan makes the point that choral music is "literally man-made in every respect," thereby pointing to the necessity for a conductor's humanness in accomplishing a musical statement.*

The performance of choral music as well know it in this country today is of comparatively recent origin. We are grateful for the pioneering efforts of the first American composers—William Billings, John Antes, Stephen Foster, Horatio Parker and others. We know that there were choral organizations who presented concerts at an early date in Boston, Philadelphia, Cincinnati and New York. Whether they came to these shores as hopeful emigrants or unwilling victims of the slave trade, thousands of newcomers brought their songs with them and composed others which told of suffering and joy, disaster or triumph. Yet, choral activity as it now exists began in America only about a half-century ago with the "discovery" of music which could be sung without accompaniment. The "a cappella choir" was primarily responsible for the great interest in choral music which has flourished in America for the past four or five decades.

Because choral singing was to some extent a new form of musical expression in the years before World War II, those who were responsible for its development used most of their time to explore the new and exciting scores which came from publishers. They also designed a basic methodology to solve rehearsal and organizational problems. *Choral repertoire and choral techniques*—these were the topics mentioned most frequently in the articles and textbooks of the time and which served as subjects for discussion or demonstration by the choral giants of the period: Peter Lutkin, Father William J. Finn, John Finley Williamson, F. Melius Christiansen and others.

After the conclusion of the war, choral leaders concentrated their attention upon problems of tone. How large or small a tone—should ensemble singers employ vibrato and if so to what extent—how was the high and low range of the voice to be developed—what was a proper definition of the term "tone quality"? These were the issues which now called forth debate and controversy. Which vowel was the most effective for constructing a beautiful choral blend? In what man-

119

ner should a tenor sing the notes above the staff and the altos those which fall below middle C? In what respect was the production of choral tone related to the singing of pitch consonants or dipthongs, to matching vowel sounds, to phrasing, breathing, support, interpretation, choice of repertoire, etc.? During this period a conductor believed strongly that his choice of a basic tone production for his chorus and his understanding of a favorite pedagogy to achieve tonal goals were the most important musical tasks to which he could address himself.

What was to be the next assignment? The choral world suddenly discovered style and performance practice. There *was* a way to sing Palestrina differently from Brahms! We learned that changes in the interpretation of one piece from another were occasioned by an understanding of many exciting facts relating to compositional styles. There had to be a consideration of the length and shape and consistency of the phrases. One was concerned with the use of particular instruments or none at all for purposes of accompaniment. There was sometimes the obvious desire of a composer for ornamentation of particular passages. A conductor needed to think about the nature of pitch and choice of tempo which was historically sound; he dealt with the formal elements of the composition, with counterpoint and harmony, sonority and the size of performing forces, with texture and sequence, contrast and climax. The conductor who worked for authentic performances was obliged to concern himself with such matters as the employment of the concertato principle and with the use of terrace dynamics in contrast to calling for crescendo and diminuendo as interpretive devices. In the light of his musical setting how did the composer view the text? What were forces other than musical which influenced the writing of the composer: nationalistic, literary, economic, political, theological, etc.? All of these and other additional factors had to do with the unique manner by which a composer expressed his ideas and with the way a conductor was to recreate them in sound. Finally, every well-intentioned director faced the truth that his preconceived techniques concerning tone and interpretation, attack and release, rhythm, balance, blend and intonation—all were changed to some degree by principles of style and performance practice.

So it was that during the fifty years or so that choral activity has been an important means of musical expression in America, professional leaders who have had the responsibility for the growth and development of ensemble singing were concerned first with organizational rehearsal, and interpretive techniques and with finding an acceptable repertoire; with utilizing a pedagogy which insured a desirable tone quality; finally, with the proper rendition of a composition according to authentic stylistic principles and performance practice.

What of the present? Has the study of scores, of vocal pedagogy, of acoustics and aesthetics—have technique and methodology and style—made for choral experiences which are exciting and successful? Are those who perform and those who listen genuinely moved by a combining of all of the elements in choral singing to produce results which are powerful and yet which defy exact definition?

No . . . It must be said that too often and perhaps more frequently than we care to admit, choral performance in these times is dull and lifeless. The spark is missing. Communication is often talked about but too seldom is achieved. The artificial and the synthetic take the place of what is real and valid. How does this happen?

Is this a partial answer? Is it true that some of our choral leaders, like many who have responsibilities for government and business, for church, family and other contemporary institutions, look to a combination of organization and technical know-how to find the solution for every issue? Dare we forget that when human beings are an important part of any venture, a mechanical approach to problem solving may be somewhat helpful but usually brings only limited results?

This is particularly true of choral music—perhaps more so than with any other form of artistic expression. Choral music literally is man-made in every respect. Its content is a combination of sounds which we call "words" by which are described or portrayed man's thoughts and judgments—his emotions, feelings, and experiences. When these verbal expressions are joined in an orderly fashion with musical elements of melody, rhythm, and harmony, they are given additional dimensions of pitch and sound. These musical factors also are responsible for a continuing renaissance of aesthetic experiences.

All of this is quite familiar to any choral person. However, he tends to forget that his music is an unusual kind of artistic expression because here ideas are born and sensed only with the union of *music and words*. Also, he must remind himself of the great differences which are encountered in preparing a chorus to sing in contrast with what is asked of a vocalist. He should understand that ensemble singing calls for special techniques, some of which are different from and others a compromise with individual vocal method. Armed with a variety of procedures which depend for their selection upon his taste, knowledge, and experience, he should attempt to secure from his singers a unified sound or response or concept. Too often, however, conductors fail to secure performances which are exciting and significant because the very procedures which they may use successfully to reach aesthetic goals tend to stultify and destroy imaginative and creative powers that are resident in an individual mind and spirit. So we ask our choruses for parrot-like phrasing in place of individual thought, and a unified tone instead of a personal sound. From our singers we insist upon concentration upon the details of the score rather than a utilization of ideas which motivate an individual response to music. As a result, that which a singer perceives in a score may be only par-

Choral music literally is man-made in every respect. Its content is a combination of sounds which we call "words," by which are described or portrayed man's thoughts and judgments—his emotions, feelings, and experiences. When these verbal expressions are joined in an orderly fashion with musical elements of melody, rhythm, and harmony they are given additional dimensions of pitch and sound.

121

tially true, and partial truth is but one step removed from that which is false. Also, if a hodge-podge of illconceived ideas is thrown out to a group of listeners, this is distressingly poor material to be communicated by a chorus or to be comprehended by its audience. As they listen, they may perceive some aesthetic values and appreciate formal elements in the score, but the complete meaning of the music which comes alive only with the imaginative understanding of conductor and singers is lost.

Let it be clearly understood that this is not an argument for a revival of the doctrine of affections or an attempt to formulate a new theory of the relativity of emotion and choral music. Neither is the claim made that in some mysterious fashion there is a power locked up in words. Rather it is suggested that in these days when we are very much aware of the emphasis upon the individual man and woman, boy or girl—when the study of personality for two decades has been at the very center of psychological research—when the techniques of communication absorb the interest of the business, artistic and professional worlds—then there must be something here of value for our own leadership to ponder. Perhaps this is to be the next sphere of activity for the choral world.

We must never forget that choral music depends upon individuals to provide every element in its creative process. Since the thought and imagination and talent of conductor and singer are able to alter each aspect of group singing, including vocal and interpretive technique, we must believe that there can be a personal equation which influences every factor in choral endeavor. Yet, in spite of the apparent validity of this statement, conductors who are interested enough to explore or to practice with the "personal element" in choral singing are comparatively few in number.

The dictionary defines "personal equation" in these terms: "the characteristics of a person as they tend to cause variation in observation, judgment and reasoning."[1] It is obvious that in a choral situation the conductor is primarily responsible for any changes in the "characteristics" of the singers. Yet, some leaders will continue to place their faith only in an impersonal methodology which has been used many times. Others will say with great conviction, "I am not the kind of person who feels comfortable when I am involved with the singers in my chorus." Then there are those who speak at length on the time factor and how this interferes with doing all that they wish to do in their rehearsals. (If time always is a limiting factor, how then do they claim to be musicians?) However, the single most important reason for the reluctance of a conductor to work with and to motivate individuals in

---

[1] *The American Heritage of the English Language*. New York: The American Heritage Publishing Company, 1969.

122

his chorus is his realization that if he is to initiate and to keep alive the processes of communication, he begins by making changes in himself.

The dictionary reminds us that the word "person" comes from the Latin "persona"—meaning "mask." Also, the word "persona" as used by psychologists refers to "the role that a person assumes in order to display his conscious intentions to himself and to others."[2] With the possible exception of an actor or a singer, it would seem that a choral conductor is tempted by the opportunities for role playing, for being "other than his real self," which are afforded to few others. Consider. In the exercise of his duties he is literally in front of his chorus or the public at almost all times. His words, his gestures and his procedures are law for his chorus. He feels keen competition, from his colleagues; much of his motivation comes from the applause of an admiring audience, from ratings received in festival or competition, and from the subjective evaluation of committee, minister or administrator. Unless he is brave enough to tape or to record his rehearsals and performances, his judgments become the extension of his desires. Very seldom does he find himself in a situation where he may discuss his problems with those who are his equals in knowledge and experience. Little wonder that he first asks for and eventually demands obedience from his chorus and expects respect from his audience. It is hardly surprising that before too long the personal pronoun becomes supreme: "*My* repertoire—*My* tempo—*My* choir."

In contrast to this unfortunate picture, consider that occasional leader who knows that some of his personal traits will need exploration and change if he expects to have positive communication with his singers. He is aware that differences in personalities and objectives among all choral conductors allow him to continue with his use of favorite techniques. He expects that his methods and results will be different from those of his colleagues. On the other hand, he accepts the premise that his profession will make unusual personal demands if he decides to draw upon the full potential of the individuals in his chorus.

Therefore, he is ready to evaluate these traits within himself:

Is he *honest*—an *optimistic realist—calm—industrious—patient—imaginative*—properly *curious* about individuals?

Is he endowed with a *sense of humor* including ability to laugh at himself?

Is he moved by *beauty* in all of its manifestations?

Can he *inspire*? (This does not call necessarily for a dramatic or dynamic personality.)

Does he *recognize* and accept the *worth* and *merit* of all human beings?

---

[2] *Ibid.*

We must never forget that choral music depends upon individuals to provide every element in its creative process. Since the thought and imagination and talent of conductor and singer are able to alter each aspect of group singing, including vocal and interpretive technique, we must believe that there can be a personal equation which influences every factor in choral endeavor.

123

Does he *listen*?

If he is willing to learn from others, he will relate and identify with them.

In a chapter which he contributes to a symposium titled *Personal Problems And Psychological Frontiers*,[3] E. K. Schwartz answers these two important questions: first, "What are the signs of personal maturity?" Schwartz says that maturity is founded upon a respect for mutual agreement as the basis of all human relations. There must be love of human beings which is coupled with a love of justice. This provides the foundation for equality, and personal equality and personal worth are intertwined. Maturity also presupposes tolerance for change as well as opposition to rigidity.

Then, Schwartz makes this second query—"What are the psychological characteristics of a mature person?" He has great inner and outer awareness. He can work and plan and struggle and be creative. Hurts are easily overcome and hostility quickly done away with. There is empathy—the capacity to identify with others and to put oneself in the other person's position. "It is the opposite of an egocentric view; it is the allocentric, the feeling centering about how the other person feels. . . ." The mature human being has the need, the wish and the freedom to be close to others emotionally and sometimes, physically. He recognizes leadership. He has the capacity to be free, not to have to agree and yet not to be "compulsively rebellious." There is the skill and the freedom to communicate. There is never the use of status as an index of human worth or the necessity always to be dependent upon others.

Perhaps there now is the thought that this article has turned into a sermon. May we review the basic principles of this statement? We have said that with every form of human endeavor, problems arise primarily because of the lack of communicative skills. All forms of art are especially dependent upon communication for their success. Choral performance is peculiarly vulnerable since conductor and chorus are "co-performers." In a choral situation, the greatest single obstacle to proper communication is that both parties too often are engaged in playing roles instead of attempting to live as real persons. The director has the primary responsibility to "remove his mask." He does this by cultivating personal traits which help him become involved with the singers in his chorus, with his audience, and with other individuals whom he meets during his day. As he reaches the point where his chorus begins to see, hear, and experience reality in his personality and honesty in his life style, they will neither fear him nor take him for granted. Rather, they will respect him for what he knows and love him

---

[3] Schwartz, E. K., *Personal Problems and Psychological Frontiers*. New York: Sheridan House. pp. 18–24.

for what he is. Because their loneliness and fear are replaced by assurance, they are encouraged to remove their own masks, which allows valid and exciting communication to take place.

Within the limits of this paper it is not possible to list the many ways in a choral situation by which one may study and experiment with group psychology, personality awareness, and methods of communication. However, I would make some few suggestions which are based upon personal reading, observation and experiment. There is no attempt to list these by activity, chronology or order of importance.

From *The Psychology of Communication* by Jon Eisenson are taken these significant observations concerned with "speaker-listener relationships."[4]

In a choral situation the greatest single obstacle to proper communication is that both parties too often are engaged in playing roles instead of attempting to life as real persons.

(1) Individuals respond most readily when they are highly involved in the purpose of the communication.

(2) The psychology of listening equals attention followed by perception.

Attention
A listener cannot give continuous attention; it comes in spurts. Change is the most basic and significant way to secure attention.

Perception
Requires: Novelty of stimulus, repetition and definiteness of form.

(3) The importance of motivation.

Human beings normally behave in ways that will lead them toward success and achievement.

Human beings like to behave in ways that will help them to gain recognition, admiration, respect and approval.

Human beings generally act in ways that lead towards the realization of a feeling of being wanted.

Human beings seek some adventure—new experiences and zestful living. They tend to avoid boredom and monotony.

From Herbert Abelson's *Persuasion* come these axioms concerning the manner in which opinions and attitudes are changed:[5]

(1) There will be more opinion change in the desired direction if the communicator has high credibility than if he has low credibility. The communicator is seen as credible to the extent that his audience accepts him as (1) expert (2) trustworthy.

(2) The motives attributed to a communicator may affect his success in influencing others.

(3) A communicator's effectiveness is increased if he expresses some views that are also held by his audience.

(4) The more extreme the opinion change that the communicator asks for, the more actual change he is likely to get.

---

[4] Eisenson, Jon, *The Psychology of Communication*. New York: Appleton-Century-Crofts, 1963.

[5] Abelson, Herbert, *Persuasion*. New York: Springer Publishing Company, 1959. pp. 72–88.

Some subjective questions and proposals:

(1) A conductor must experiment to find the ways by which he communicates most effectively during a rehearsal. If he uses speech, does he stress logic, the pictorial, or qualities of imagination? Does he sing or play to make his points? Does he use a combination of the visual and auditory? Does the communication have form? Is he able to skip or march or dance without embarrassment to indicate rhythmic flow? Can he tell the chorus simply and with conviction how and why music moves him? Is he able to do everything in a rehearsal without being self conscious on the one hand or exploiting his personality on the other?

(2) If the conductor is attempting to teach others to be appreciative of beauty, what of his own endowment? Does he respond with enthusiasm to form and design and color—to babies and flowers and people? How long has it been since he has seen a collection of fine paintings or read a book of poetry?

(3) As the director tells his singers how and why a particular score appeals to him, he should not hesitate to "read between the lines" and make his educated guesses concerning the wishes of the composer. He will want to share with the chorus his technical and interpretive decisions. Yet, he never should insist that his singers think and feel exactly as he does. This is not possible.

(4) The conductor will make allowances for the age and experience of the chorus. Since children find it easy to live in two worlds, one which is real and the other imaginary, he takes advantage of this fact and uses it to flavor many communicative procedures. Older people depend upon associative ideas; he makes use of this trait. The conductor needs to change frequently his method and his terminology, but he should never find it necessary to change his personality.

(5) Don't make comments *only* to shock—to please in a superficial way—to hurt or to ridicule. If a conductor is considered by his chorus to be a cynic, they will doubt his sincerity when he speaks of important musical matters.

The world of persons has much meaning for the world of choral conducting. As Paul Tournier has said—"We always find time for what we are interested in. There can be few vocations more interesting than seeking to understand the human person."[6]

---

[6] Tournier, Paul, *The Meaning of Persons*. New York, Harper and Row, 1957. p. 45.

Report to the Profession

Delivered in Dallas to the 1977 national convention of the American Choral Directors Association, Swan's report admonishes choral musicians to include the three "h's": honesty, humility, and humor along with the musicianship that they are expected to possess in order to achieve excellence.

In a time when the news media bombard us daily with sensational accounts of happenings far away or near at hand, it takes a most unusual and startling report to engage our attention. Recently, I read such an item and was shaken by its significance. In the January 1977 issue of the *Music Educators Journal* as a part of his monthly report to the membership, President Robert Klotman repeated a statistic which had just been released by the Department of Health, Education and Welfare: "In the public secondary schools of this country over a period of 12 years' time, enrollments in drama courses have increased over five times, from 119,000 to 575,000 students." There was also a substantial gain in the enrollments in art education. But in music? The percentage of *all* high school students enrolled in some area of music education *declined* from 42% in 1960-61 to approximately 33% 12 years later.

Dr. Klotman went on to make this pertinent comment: "We need to ask ourselves what were we doing in teaching music that caused students to reject our activities . . . .Perhaps the procedures and ideas that were successful in the 30's and 40's became less applicable in the 60's and are even less so for the 70's and the 80's." We are probably aware that all is not well with music. But, unless we are foolish enough to believe that music as an *art form* has lost its appeal, we must accept the grim fact that the fault lies with those of us who teach, perform, and guide musical thinking, learning and activity for people of all ages and levels of experience.

I do not believe for a moment that the choral profession has been guilty of mistakes in attempting to learn all that is possible about matters of musicianship, score analysis, the conduct of rehearsals, the nature of the human instrument, interpretive procedures and the like. These topics are fundamental; they have been and will continue to be important for anyone who is a teacher or performer in the choral idiom. Here in these last years of the 1970's a mastery of techniques no longer can guarantee true success. What *is* needed (and it is of vast importance) is a complete and sympathetic understanding of every *human*

We are probably aware that all is not well with music. But, unless we are foolish enough to believe that music as an **art form** *has lost its appeal, we must accept the grim fact that the fault lies with those of us who teach, perform, and guide musical thinking, learning and activity for people of all ages and levels of experience.*

being who, as a member of a chorus, is in front of us each day or each week. There must happen and happen quickly—the desire to know fully each *personality,* the biological, mental, and spiritual forces which work towards its development, and the several ways by which proper motivation can build individual happiness and self-fulfillment. Most importantly, what are the musical devices, techniques, and experiences which can help with this process of growth?

At Westridge School in Pasadena with the Alumni/Parent Glee Club, 1986

128

To teach for the complete person—to attempt to show others how to live more effectively—is not a new idea. Always, however, such an objective is a challenging one; perhaps never so much as now, when there is in this country such a feeling of division, of fragmentation, and of loss of credibility. So it is that together with many of their fellow Americans our singers think constantly these thoughts: In what and in whom may I believe? How can I rid myself of my fears and inhibitions? Who and what am I? Will I ever be of any use in this world?

What an opportunity there is here for the choral conductor! In our art we deal with words and their musical settings: symbols which together voice some of man's most beautiful and significant ideas. Further, the singing process requires that each person involved will stamp his or her song with individual creative concepts—ideas associated with color, order, beauty, balance, and truth—ideas which can be given a new and powerful dimension with the help of a conductor or teacher who communicates freely and easily with singers of all ages and accepts them as partners and co-workers in performance.

Unfortunately, with but all too few exceptions, this is not the way that it is. Any truthful observer would find it necessary to report that the members of our choruses are not the only ones who are confused and fearful—or who are caught up with role playing. *So are their leaders.* Now in our first year of teaching we may have been so timid that we hardly knew what to say to a chorus each time we stopped their singing. Some of us have never left this period of fear and frustration. But others—terribly ego-centered—have gone very far indeed in the other direction. They seem to have forgotten the full title of the recently popular psychological treatise on communication. They are sure that the name is—"I'm O.K." . . . period! They remain complete adolescents!

Have you ever considered the artificiality and phoniness of the usual musical rehearsal and performance? The conductor stands constantly in front of the chorus or the audience; he or she is always in the spotlight. The very nature of a rehearsal causes us to think and to speak in negative terms to our choirs. It is: "No, no—you missed that pitch." "Your blend is terrible." "Sopranos, you are flat." "Precision in attack is quite ragged." "You don't sing with the proper quality." "*No, don't*—that's bad," etc. Sometimes it seems that we are so busy trying to promote ourselves that we can hardly afford the time even to learn the names of those who sing in our chorus, let alone make the attempt to understand the thinking and the life styles of our choristers. We become obsessed with a goal of making the programs which we conduct better in their sound and content than those performed by our principal competitor who lives either across town or across the state.

The singing process requires that each person involved will stamp his or her song with individual creative concepts—ideas associated with color, order, beauty, balance, and truth—ideas which can be given a new and powerful dimension with the help of a conductor or teacher who communicates freely and easily with singers of all ages and accepts them as partners and co-workers in performance.

Candidly, we are somewhat jealous and fearful of this person and so we disparage the work he or she does until we meet together at a festival or conference. We thrive on *praise* regardless of its source, and yet we cannot seem to abide the least bit of negative criticism.

In some ways it seems to me at times that this is all rather pseudo and artificial and even downright dishonest. Where is music? Where is beauty? Where is living? Perhaps these nonsensical verses may help to make my point:

⟨ *Conductors We Have Known* ⟩

I knew a musician conductor named Bard
Who worked every singer too hard;
All his tempos were fast
And each tone was a blast—
At 40 he's in a graveyard.

A conductor called Percival Bassett
Redundantly labored each facet—
For hours he's talk and in he would walk
While his players just sat and were tacet.

She didn't know music, from students she shrank,
From the back of her stand she would peek;
Many times every year she was flattened by fear,
Then would stay in her bed for a week.
With the counsel of others, she chose all the songs—
Her opinions? There wasn't a sound;
Such a person as this most surely belongs
In some spot where no music is found.
"My chorus! My concert!" to speak such self-praise
Is foolish indeed. For thus does one mock
Those musicians who practice for many long days,
The genius of Mozart and Bach.

And this one for teachers in the grades and junior high schools to think about:

Was Mr. Smith ever a boy?
Did he know how to swim, to run, to enjoy
All the things that are super? The ball
In the basket from 20 feet out? To call
For a dog and have him come running? To make
A neat biplane with love and with care? Then wake
All the neighbors with its fearful noise!
Was Mr. Smith one of a gang of real boys?

Does Mr. Smith know that its super to read
About athletic records or traveling at speed
That is faster than lightening? Has he ever heard

The love in a dog's bark, the sound of a bird?
Has he felt the crackling of leaves between toes
When he walks thro' the deep woods, and then as he goes
Further and further until there's no sun—
And it's almost as though the night had begun?

Mr. Smith leads our chorus and sometimes it seems
That he never has had any wonderful dreams
Of interesting places and people and things
That are found in our school books. Whenever *he* sings
It's not very pretty, and we look away
And wish that the music would stop for today.

We boys like to sing—we've already found
That our voices together make a wonderful sound.
But if we must look at Mr. Smith's face
We wish we were in some far away place.
He doesn't look happy as he tries to be coy—
I wonder—Was Mr. Smith ever a boy?

A few moments ago we reviewed the various emphases which have interested American choral conductors over the past 50 years. This kind of evolutionary growth also has been true of the science of psychology. However, as with music when new ideas and procedures came into being, none of the great psychological truths were abandoned. Rather, there has been an adding to of knowledge; not a complete displacement of one approach by another. This was particularly true of the phenomenon which we call "motivation"—a most important part of rehearsal. The so-called "common-sense" theory of motivation first conceived of behavior as being directed towards the sources of *satisfaction*. At a later time, William James, the father of psychology, believed that motivation was the same as one's *conscious volition* to proceed towards a goal. Freud introduced the importance of unconscious motives. Then followed the experiments of Thorndyke, Talwan, and Woodworth which dealt with purposive behavior—and the importance of the achievement motive which asserted that true motivation comes from pleasure in any activity which is successful.

To these and other valid approaches to psychological problems have been added some provocative ideas concerning motivational procedures. Abraham H. Maslow was the brilliant and very personable proponent of the ideas advanced by this newest school of psychological thought. I believe that his ideas can furnish exciting answers for many problems which we encounter with our students.

Maslow begins with the proposal that the true teacher knows that one great and ultimate goal of education is to help a person become a human being—as fully human as he or she can be. A healthy teacher is neither sick physically nor mentally. Thus, teacher-student relationships for this healthy person consist of a pleasant collaboration rather than a clash of wills or authority or dignity which is easily threatened,

Five statements which define the purposes and practices of our unique vocation: (1) WE BELIEVE IN the acceptance of our scholarly and musical responsibilities for each score which we propose to conduct. (2) WE BELIEVE IN the joyous, continuing search for the central idea—the form, the spirit, the truth to be found in every serious musical composition. (3) WE BELIEVE IN the necessity for each of us to become a master of technique including a knowledge of vocal procedures by which choirs are taught to sing with beauty. (4) WE BELIEVE IN the employment of standards for study, motivation, and rehearsal which lead to EXCELLENCE in teaching and performance. (5) WE BELIEVE IN: FAITH— in ourselves and in our singers, HOPE—that those who listen to our choirs will understand what the music is saying, and LOVE—which by musical means combines beauty and art, form and sound, the personal and the objective, release and fulfillment, appreciation and understanding love working through the power of music to transform lives for an hour or a year or a lifetime.—**"The Nashville Symposium: 'A Cause for Celebration,'—"** *The Choral Journal,* **October 1983.**

compared to a natural simplicity which is *not* easily threatened. The insistence on remaining as realistically human as, say, a plumber or a carpenter, and the giving up of the attempt to be *omniscent* in front of the group, creates an atmosphere in the rehearsal in which suspicion, defensiveness, anxiety, and hostility tend to disappear.

Like most psychologists, Maslow believes that all humans have basic needs which must be satisfied before anyone can become a completely healthy person. However, he asserts that these needs are not all equally important. So-called "lower needs" are more tangible, localized, and limited than are the "higher needs"—the latter are later evolutionary developments. Further, higher needs require positive environmental conditions to make their gratification possible.

The starting point for motivation theory is with the so-called physiological drives. These are the most potent of all needs; for the one who is hungry, no other interest exists but food. But, when there is plenty of bread, other and higher needs immediately arise; at first, the group which may be characterized as the "safety needs," that is, security, stability, protection, freedom from fear, the need for order, etc. If both the physiological and safety needs are gratified there next emerge *love* and *affection* and the need or feeling to belong. Finally, there is a need for self-respect and for the esteem of others which may be defined in terms of status, recognition, attention, and the like. Satisfaction by way of self-esteem leads to assurance and confidence, the belief that one is useful in the world.

While a basically satisfied person no longer *requires* love and respect, belongingness, or to be confident and assured, yet he or she develops a new discontent and restlessness *unless* involved in doing what he or she is fitted for. A poet must write—an artist *must* paint—and musicians *must* make music if they are to be at peace with the person within. What we *can* be we *must* be! This is what Maslow calls the movement towards "self-actualization" or "self-fulfillment"—never completely realized until we are adults—but hopefully having been motivated towards that goal during our younger years. The new humanistic philosophy has generated a concept of learning which holds that the function of education ultimately is the self-actualization of a person, the assisting of one to become the best that he or she is able to become.

How does one know that he or she is a self-actualizing person? After some considerable time spent in investigation, Maslow suggests these clues. He asserts that self-fulfilling people are involved in causes outside of, or other than themselves. They work at something which is precious and important to them. They devote their lives to the ultimate values which are intrinsic, that is, which cannot be reduced to anything more ultimate. What are some of these values? *Truth, reality, justice, beauty, aliveness, uniqueness, order, simplicity, grace and effortlessness, playfulness* (meaning joy and amusement and exhuberance), and *self-sufficiency.* To self-actualize, one becomes fully human and forgets one's poses, defenses, shyness, etc. *Oneself* emerges—not the *someone else*—that is, the parent or child or adolescent who may be within us. If we must be different to be right, we dare to do so. After identifying them, we give up all our defenses.

Let us think now of ourselves as we work with our choirs. How does one grow towards the goal of self-fulfillment and at the same time attempt to meet the needs of our singers? I believe that in addition to a sound sense of musicianship a conductor must strive to live the 3 "h's": *honesty, humility,* and *humor.* Further, the choice of repertoire and the planning of rehearsals should result in the *learning* of and *about all* involved in the musical score, instead of rehearsing music only to perform it. Basic essentials in choral music should be emphasized as in the past, but the approaches to achievement should be made as a cooperative venture with the members of our choirs. A conductor must be willing to experiment in the attempt to find the best ways to communicate with the chorus. Don't confine yourself to the usual procedure—the everlasting talk, talk, talk! Observe, know, and trust your singers. Thank them individually and not collectively whenever possible. They are real people, too.

Our people need and deserve more of a personal involvement with the learning process. What is in the score and *why* it is there must be as important as *how* to perform it! Where possible, answers should be relevant to the entire spectrum of music as an art form and, in many situations, to experiences found in our day-to-day living.

If procedures are used intelligently and are planned with the cooperative strength of each chorus member, all will receive insight concerning the ultimate values of beauty, honesty, order, and the other intrinsic virtues which receive illustration in the text and musical setting of every worthwhile choral composition.

I treasure memories of many musical experiences and have had the opportunity to know some of the world's greatest choral musicians. These men were singularly alike in several respects. They worked hard. They were not bothered by petty and insignificant problems. Instead, their lives were lived simply and with great joy. They found beauty all about them in painting, flowers, poetry, and a thousand other places; most importantly, they loved both people and music with a tremendous zeal.

I am thankful for these memories of the past, but, as one who continues to be both curious and realistically optimistic, I look *forward* to a time when music in its performance as in its composition will be relevant to all of the processes of living. There will be mutual respect

> *I believe in addition to a sound sense of musicianship a conductor must strive to live the 3 "h's":* **honesty, humility,** *and* **humor.**

133

between leader and singers, an honest simplicity in the expression of personality, and an acceptance of the premise that, in comprehending all of the beauty in *music*, we also learn much about the beauty and truth and goodness which continue to exist in this world.

The Choral Musician
In a Changing World

Delivered to the graduates of Westminster Choir College in Princeton Chapel, Princeton, New Jersey, on May 20, 1977. Swan received an honorary degree from the college on this day.

This is a season of the year when throughout America thousands of seniors like you, in cap and gown, sit through exercises much like these this morning. Unless I am completely wide of the mark, the graduates of 1977 anticipate their tomorrows with a hope for satisfaction and success which the future may bring. But this desire, (and how well we know this) is tempered by a fear of the unknown. For the world is changing and the tempo is *vivace*. So much of what we see and hear and feel in life about us is downbeat, it's negative.

The musical scene reflects these unsettled times. Symphonies and operatic organizations continue to have their problems with administrative procedures, finances, and choice of repertoire. In many districts of the country, and I imagine some of you know this all right, rising costs have led to partial or complete cancellation of music classes by school boards and administrators. Some of our churches admit to declining membership. Those charged with the responsibility for a program of church music too often have to struggle in the midst of almost impossible circumstances primarily because of the decline in the volunteer spirit and an unwillingness to sacrifice time and energy for the good of the group. It all makes for a very gloomy picture.

But hasn't such always been the case? For those who lived at a particular time in history, have not matters been constantly in a state of flux? We could mention the name of many musicians who found their world less than a wonderful place in which to live. Think of Bach and Mozart. Hugo Distler, St. Augustine, Beethoven, Peter Warlock, Bartok, and Schoenberg, and thousands of others, many of them unknown, insofar as fame or prestige are concerned. The important thing for us is this: What kept them going? A few lines from a letter of Schubert gives us one clue. He writes: "We suppose that happiness attaches to any place (Westminster, perhaps?) where we were once happy whereas it is only within ourselves. So I was first disappointed where I work. But now I am better able to find happiness and tranquility within myself. You will see evidence of this in the fact that I have already composed a long sonata and variations on a theme of my own, both for piano duet. The variations are winning quite exceptional applause in Vienna."

It must be obvious to each of us that the world never can be a kind of place that will please everyone. But there will continue to be those *thousands* who believe that with the power of creative endeavor, people and events and circumstances can always be altered for the better. Paul

In rehearsal at Occidental College for a European tour in 1968. The Occidental Glee Club won three prizes that year at the Eisteddfod at Slagoffesh, Wales.

Henry Lang says it in this fashion: "The greatness of the modern creative artist depends on whether he or she has the power to overcome the volcanic upheaval of the times without being consumed."

I must assume that anyone who has chosen a profession which is in arts is concerned both with aspects of beauty and also with people is anxious to be counted with all the men and women who do what they can to improve life in this world. The first step in such a challenging process begins with one's self. So I put the question to you graduates, as forcefully as possible: *how effective a choral musician do you plan to be?* After four years or so at this college, and you've probably been thinking of this kind of answer, you certainly know something about beats and blend and balance, rhythmic vitality and rehearsal plans, the Renaissance and Romantic periods, diction and dynamics and all the rest of the skills which are necessary for the success of a choral musician. But though all of this equipment is important, you won't make it as a conductor until there have been other kinds of education and growth and experience.

Let me explain. Shakespeare characterized men as living through seven ages, each one a period of activity based upon chronological time. Musically speaking, I've observed that every successful choral musician appears to live and work through five stages—and these are not dependent upon one's years. Now some of you already have conducted choruses in a professional situation, while others are yet to have their first encounter. It's a fearful day when you face a choir in your first professional job for the first time, and to some degree this uneasy feeling lasts not only for the first time but for several months. You find yourself in front of the chorus, the members of the choir eye you furtively as they sing and you suddenly panic. What will you say to them when the sound stops? When they stop singing? Your mind races; you can't concentrate on what's happening. You're dimly aware that the accompanist, if you are lucky enough to have one, is correcting the mistakes of the singers. You think desperately, Now what was it that you were told to do back there at Westminster, by Mr. Simpson or Mr. Shrock or Dr. Flummerfelt? Finally the chorus reaches the end of the piece and looks up expectantly. For a split second you're tongue-tied, and then you gasp weakly, "That's very nice, choir, now do it again, a little more softly."

Now this is what I call a *first stage of experience.* Alas, some conductors never leave this stage. But what usually happens next? There's a complete shift in procedures. For instead of not knowing what to say, *the second stage* musician hardly can wait for the chorus to stop singing so that he or she can talk. And talk is heard incessantly, for all of a sudden our budding genius has become an authority on almost any musical subject. For example: The rehearsal is stopped so that the conductor may correct the sopranos for using too bright a tone on page 2. As the director finally stops for breath, there is a remembrance that on page 11 the tenors sang under the pitch for a line or two. Accordingly, the tenors receive a short lecture on intonation and learning intervals properly. Now it's the altos turn, for they sang much too breathily on page 5, and since the composer is Brahms, the conductor proclaims knowingly that the piece needs much more color in its interpretation. Interpretation? Oh, suddenly the conductor thinks, "What do I know about interpretation?" Style! That's it! Romantic music! Yes, tempo rubato! And here we go again with the conductor telling the chorus almost all that is known concerning the why's and wherefore's of tempo rubato. By this time, the reason why the choir was stopped in the first place has been completely forgotten. The tragedy is, that too many choral musicians never seem to get beyond this stage in growth and experience.

What is *the third stage*? The third stage I call the adolescent stage when the conductor is intrigued with sound, and his/her ability to control it at will. We love the power we hold over our choruses. We play with the music, and we particularly like it when perhaps some of the elderly members of our congregation or our audience, come up and say, "Oh, Mr. Swan, I love your hands! Your fingers are so graceful." And we say, "Thank you very much." And we think so too! And so we love to make the chorus crescendo, and diminuendo, and with a flick of the finger, change from the *hmmm* to an *ooh* and an *ahhh*. And, of course, this influences the kind of music we pick, because we like music that has all these changes in it. I don't know how it is here in New Jersey but in Southern California, there are many conductors of both sexes who are still living in the adolescent stage.

The fourth stage of growth finds conductors depending almost completely, upon the teaching of others for all of his knowledge, methods, choice of literature, and all the rest. America has been and is blessed with many great choral conductors and teachers. But can we hold them responsible for all that we know and do? If we imitate them too closely, we are lost. We can spend every summer attending workshops taught by experts and can memorize all the rules, but there comes a time when a conductor must know enough so that he can throw away the rule book. When this happens, a conductor has reached a *fifth stage*, and is well on the way to becoming a true artist.

What we're saying is that in order to cope with a changing world, you must start with yourself. You will go through stages of development which may be awkward and sometimes self defeating. Hopefully, you can become a musician who is independent in thought and procedure, but you have become successful in part by discovering that in this profession, one must make compromises, decisions, and choices. The balancing of one factor against another is important in many musical situations. It can be largely responsible for the choice of your own lifestyle. What are you going to emphasize?

The effectiveness of our teaching, and the influential power that is inherent in music was and is judged on the basis, sometimes, of the number of superior ratings received by an ensemble in festivals or contests. And there are some states not too far from this one where this happens all the time.—
"Humanistic Education," Little Rock, 1979.

Our responsibility as choral musicians does not stop with the teaching of music. We must find time and energy for thought and study so that we can help teach people how to live. And what an opportunity! A true teacher knows that one great and ultimate goal of education *is* to help a person become a human being, as fully human as he or she can be. A healthy teacher or choral musician, if you like, is neither sick physically or mentally. Thus teacher-student relationships for this healthy person consist of a pleasant collaboration rather than a clash of wills, or authority or dignity which is easily threatened, compared to a natural simplicity which is not easily threatened. The basic needs of hunger, safety, love, affection, and the feeling that one belongs, must be satisfied before anyone can become a completely healthy person. How many people will you run into who feel that they don't belong to anything, that no one cares?

After these five stages through which most of you will go, what else is left? Continue, I beg of you, to find great joy and inspiration in the art which you propose to serve. This is the way Robert Schumann felt about about music. He said: "In every time there reigns a secret language of kindred spirits. Tighten the circle you who belong to it in order that the truth in art may shine forth more and more brightly, everywhere spreading joy and peace." And I imagine many of you know these words from Martin Luther's pen: "I have always loved music. Those who have mastered this art are of good stuff. They are fit for any task. Music is a beautiful and glorious gift of God. I would not give up what little I know about music for something else which I might have in greater abundance." Arnold Schoenberg said: "I've always had a passion for teaching. I've always felt the urge to discover what can most help beginners and how they can be made thoroughly acquainted with the technical, intellectual and ethical of our art. How to teach them that there is a morality of art and why one must never cease to foster it and always combat to the utmost any attempt to violate it."

The choral musician in a changing world: Change with the world but not too much. Find the satisfaction, the strength and the assurance within yourself. Always have this special feeling which you have for your choice of this art. Never let it be lost. I hope that the credo, your credo, will contain rhythms which are vital and strong, harmonies which will unite all who sing or live them, and your own unique and beautiful melody which will be filled with joy and delight and endure to the end of time. God bless you.

Our responsibility as choral musicians does not stop with the teaching of music. We must find time and energy for thought and study so that we can help teach people how to live.

The Making of the Presidents, 1979

This address, requested by the American Choral Directors Association, was presented at a leadership retreat at Lawton, Oklahoma on June 16, 1979. It was published in the May 1980 issue of The Choral Journal.

For the past few weeks, Katherine Swan and I have been reading the best seller by Theodore H. White titled, *In Search of History.* The book is fascinating in its content, so much so that we have remarked several times that an autobiography of this kind carries a most appropriate title. White was a first-hand witness of the Chinese revolution, of the Japanese surrender in Tokyo Bay after World War II, of the Berlin Airlift, and of the political scene in America for the past 25 years. He was friend or acquaintance to the great in many countries, including Mao Tse Tung and Chou En-lai in China, Generals Lou Stillwell, Claire Chennault, and Douglas McArthur, and Presidents Dwight Eisenhower and Richard Nixon.

In the writing of his book, White restates a theme which is familiar to all of us. He believes that the great movements of history are the result of numberless events which take place every hour of every day and which, as they occur, seem at first to have no relationship to each other.

There is an analogy here with the story of ACDA. All of us are acquainted with the accounts of the founding of this organization and its amazing growth in membership and activity over a comparatively short period of time. Like Mr. White's history, much of what ACDA has accomplished began as a series of separate ideas, formulated and discussed over the years and finally put into action by groups of earnest and involved choral conductors. These became the means by which ACDA has grown to reach its present successful state. These ideas have given us our history; we now see them in a pattern which has determined the ways that this professional organization functions to better serve its members.

There is another analogy which exists between White's search for his intellectual roots and the story of ACDA. His desire to observe, and even to be a part of, history eventually led him to concentrate upon a study of four American presidential campaigns. He was impressed with the obvious fact that, in the selection of their leaders, the people of this country decided upon their economic, political, and social future for years to come. Their decisions affected not only the United States but the entire world.

The analogy is plain for all to see. The ACDA membership has chosen you for their leaders—thoughtful men and women who constantly demonstrate their concern for the well being of ACDA. How fortunate we have been to see the positive results of the reorganization of staff and publication procedures and the careful manner in which finances have been budgeted and dispersed. The growth in membership is greater than the most optimistic of predictions, and our latest source for self-congratulation is the dedication of this splendid headquarters facility. The end result is a membership which continues almost unanimously to be enthusiastic and vitally interested in the affairs of their professional organization. We have a fine image among choral people everywhere. "To belong to ACDA is the thing to do." So, all is positive and upbeat, and a happy future is certain.

But, is it? Have we forgotten so soon the impact made in the past on our comfortable lives by Sputnik and Vietnam and in the present by OPEC and the problems of nuclear energy? Our choral music is very much a part of the contemporary educational scene. And, at the present time, educational philosophy and procedure, honored in the past by the American people, in many places is now disparaged and criticized in negative terms. The character of all of education is being debated and restructured and, in some areas, is undergoing radical change.

Perhaps for the first time in history a large segment of the American public is suspicious of the teaching profession. Music, together with the arts and much of the rest of the academic curriculum, suffers from the present mood. Any discussion of music—of how the art will fare in the future—must proceed with the understanding that tentative conclusions will be conditioned by what happens eventually to all of educational philosophy and procedure.

Are we who teach and administer educational programs responsible for the way that one public sector views education? In a recent issue of *The Saturday Review*, Norman Cousins makes these unsettling statements:

> The saga of the taxpayers revolt as was to be expected has not ended with the demand for reductions and refunds. . . . Now the stage is set for the dimantling of hard fought gains in the fulfillment of society's responsibility to its citizens. . . . Education is now being marked out as the first casualty. Pent up prejudices against teachers and teaching are popping out all over. The arts are being derided as secondary to what is believed to be the genuine purpose of education. The genuine purpose of education, many people believe is namely, to teach people to do things *for which they will be paid*. At a time like this the real

failure of education becomes apparent: education has failed to educate about education. It has failed to provide adequate understanding of the centrality of education in a creative society. Schools have somehow failed to get across the biggest truth of all about learning, that its purpose is to unlock the human mind and to develop it into an organ capable of thought! Conceptual thought, analytical thought, sequential thought. Such thought is essential, not just for making a living, but for placing a proper value on the enjoyment of living . . .

The place of the fine arts in education is being attacked on practical grounds, but it may well be that education in the arts is the most practical function of education today . . .

One of the biggest needs of the school is not to teach people to do things, but to help them to understand what they are doing. Nothing is easier than to create a society of people in motion. Nothing is more difficult than to keep them from going nowhere . . . The big trick is to get them to think about creating better options for themselves and the next generation. The making of things, useful though they may be, is not as essential as the making of choices . . .

How do we go about educating our public officials and the general public itself in the care and feeding of civilization? How do we instruct them in the anatomy of creativity? Purely in the long range educational terms, a well rounded education is the best investment a society can make in its own future . . . [1]

Mr. Cousins gives us much to think about as he speaks of education in *general terms*. But, what of the *music educator*? How is our branch of the profession behaving during these difficult days? Lois Harrison of the University of Oregon says that we are guilty of making too many mistakes. Here are some taken from her list:

(1) Instead of working on sequential learning strategies we become masters of entertainment.
(2) We try to avoid remedial work for children who cannot achieve immediate results in music.
(3) By encouraging only talented students, we come close to saying that musicians are created genetically and are not influenced by their environments.
(4) Instead of develping independent, aware musicians in our performing groups, we remain content to conduct obedient robots, often by rote.
(5) We allow concerts to be our sole contact with the public.
(6) We search for new materials with novelty attraction rather than musical depth.
(7) We do not attempt research in our classrooms and pay little attention to that conducted by other educators.

Professor Harrison finishes her statement by saying, "You may be bristling because you can cite many music educators guiltless of these abuses. If so, there maybe hope for us yet. But we must help each other

[1] Norman Cousins, "The Taxpayers' Revolt: Act Two," *Saturday Review*, Sept. 16, 1978, p. 56.

Any discussion of music — of how the art will fare in the future — must proceed with the understanding that tentative conclusions will be conditioned by what happens eventually to all of educational philosophy and procedure.

get our houses in order while we still have some public school music programs left."[2]

But, perhaps the greatest mistake that is made by the music educator is in confusing the public relations aspect of music with the actual, real, or aesthetic importance and function of the art. As is true of many things, when a particular goal is stressed too strongly over a long period of time, in place of achieving a desired objective we learn that unwillingly we have changed its design and the reason for its existence. I believe that this happens many times as music educators attempt to develop their relationships with the public. Many of us are anxious to find a functional, pragmatic reason for the inclusion of performance in the school curriculum. So we hit upon *public relations*; that is, what our music does for the "image" of the school at the football game, for the local service club and the churches, and for all of those who hear our brass ensembles and chamber choirs perform 27 times during the week preceding Christmas vacation.

The effectiveness of our teaching and the influential power that is inherent in music many times is judged on the basis of the number of superior ratings received by an ensemble in festival or contest, by the size of the marching band, the exciting plans for a tour of the state, or Mexico, or Europe, or by the crowd pleasing choreography which is the outstanding feature of the Spring musical. For all of these procedures we beat the drum so strongly for the public relations aspect of music that there now are thousands on and off of our school campuses for whom public relations and music education are synonymous. If carried to extremes this entire process can amount to the prostitution of an art!

The December, 1978, issue of the *Music Educators Journal* contained several interesting statements on the present state of the marching band. I was surprised to find so many conflicting opinions in this symposium. From one article titled, "A Reflection of the Conductor," came these lines which should make us thoughtful concerning choral responsibilities and objectives. The author writes:

> If we are to take the term "exploitation" literally to mean "to use another for one's own selfish interest," then we must conclude that thousands of young musicians are indeed being exploited at athletic performances. The question is in what way and by whom are they being exploited? What is our role as teachers?
> The majority of people see the marching band serving a two-fold function. On one hand, band music serves as a spirit builder, adding to the overall aura of the contest. On the other, the band provides some entertainment during lulls in the action, particularly at halftime. . . .

---

[2] Lois N. Harrison, "We Make Too Many Mistakes," *Music Power*. (Washington, D.C.: Music Educators National Conference), March 1978.

With a general public to entertain and satisfy, marching bands, quite understandably, perform pop or rock literature that will be recognizable to the audience. . . .

The larger percentage of (band) programs include a marching band that performs at games and may or may not compete during the football season. In most programs, the concert season begins, at the least, when football performances are completed. . . .

We must admit that athletic performances are here to stay. Just what, then, is the proper direction in which to move? No matter what direction we choose, the one criterion we must use has to do with the effect our program has on the music education of our students. If we allow our own self-interests to interfere with students' musicality, then we are as exploitive as the audiences for whom we perform. . . .

Enthusiasm for a marching band at halftime of the big game will most certainly be of a finer pitch and will be much more vocal and demonstrative than at a formal concert. Although most people will relate to Star Wars more readily than to the Hindemith *Symphony in B*[^b] *Major* this does not make the former a better piece of music. . . .

It is only through the upgrading and sophistication of our concert bands that the art of music can be not only maintained but nurtured. If we are truly dedicated musicians, we will do everything in our power

Howard and Katherine with Dr. Richard Gilman, President of Occidental College, on the occasion of the awarding of an honorary degree

to ensure the growth of the art we so dearly love and will see that nothing deters that growth.[3]

Writing in the April, 1979, issue of *The Choral Journal*, Sandra Cryder says that a "School choir serves a function similar to that of the marching band as a public relations group for the school. A broader base of support can be gained and that means money for our school programs. What administration is going to scoff at public support and money?" Ms. Cryder asserts that many higher education music programs are "esoteric." The study of music "helps our students expand as musicians." But, "what are we giving students to prepare them for the real world of performing and teaching? Can we remain in our Ivory Tower and still be valid as educators?" She then answers her question with this somewhat astonishing statement: "Our Ivory Towers need to stand on simple but solid earth if they are to continue to exist."[4]

Here is a colleague for whom a basic objective of school music is that of entertainment with public relations and commercial overtones. She has made a definition of music for herself and her students and there are many others who support a similar point of view. However, there is a great body of Ms. Cryder's colleagues who would wonder at her use of the term "esoteric," would deny that their musical activity restricts them to an "Ivory Tower"—and who would be greatly concerned if public relations were to be considered as the principal reason for music's existence.

You who are the newly selected leaders of ACDA will find this disagreement concerning the nature of music—its being and its function—you will find that without wise and careful thought, discussion and procedure, an honest difference of opinion can become a cruel and divisive force. And there are other aspects of the contemporary scene which cause me concern and with which the ACDA must deal with in time. What are some of these?

(1) The seeming disappearance of the male singer.

(2) The lack of artistry and technical excellence in the singing of many choruses who represent the United States (and our profession) as they tour Mexico, The Orient and many European countries.

(3) The lack of "carry-over" as our singers complete their high school and college educations. Where are they?

(4) The loss of many choral music programs from the elementary and middle or junior high school level.

(5) The seeming inability of many choral conductors to choose program materials. We depend upon others to do the job for us—by review or by sponsored reading sessions.

Why are we so afraid to talk to our boys and girls about beauty? Some years ago I was conducting a festival in one of the southwest states [and at an intermission in rehearsal a young man said]: "Dr. Swan, you talked about things that we've never heard an adult talk about before, that we talk about all the time: Beauty, and what makes for beauty. And how wonderful music is. And how wonderful poetry is. And how marvelous painting is. And how beautiful it is to see a man run, or carry a football, from the standpoint of how beautifully he's formed. But until today, Dr. Swan, we've never heard an adult mention these things. So we just wanted to come a little closer and talk to you for a few minutes."—**"Humanistic Education," Little Rock, 1979.**

[3] Jack Williamson, "A Reflection of the Conductor," *Music Educators Journal.* (Volume 65, Number 4) December 1978, p. 27.

[4] Sandra Cryder, "Are Show Choirs Valid?" *The Choral Journal.* (Volume 19, Number 8), April 1979, p. 44.

146

(6) The loosening of standards in the selection of repertoire. "Quality" and "good taste" will become words without functional meaning if this trend continues.

For the past two days you have been experiencing an excellent orientation concerning the "hows" which are a part of your responsibilities; the best way to do *this*, and to accomplish *that*. I urge that in addition to the *how*, you find opportunities to deal with the *why* and the *what* and particularly with the *who*. What is to be your response to what I would consider to be the "first commandment" in the ACDA Bible? You remember: "The highest purpose of the ACDA is to encourage the finest in choral music and to promote its development in all ways including performance, composition, publication and research." Now, how do you propose to meet this challenge?

Why not make a beginning by creating your own definition of music? What does music mean to me? What is the source of its power? What are its functions? Are any of the following statements helpful as you think in terms of a philosophy of your own? Here is one:

> Music is aesthetic. It appeals to people because it possesses elements of beauty expressed both in form and sound. It cannot be defined in scientific terms, yet this is a virtue rather than a hindrance, for the ambiguous, indefinable character of music makes it an art that is important to different people for different reasons.[5]

And another:

> I like to believe that there are "3 R's" in music whether it is considered as a subject in the curriculum or a continuing experience in adult life. First, and possibly most important, is the *RECREATIVE* power of music. Secondly, there is the capacity to build a wonderful *RAPPORT* which develops as performers learn to cooperate with one another and to communicate with their audience. Finally, there is music's unique quality of *REPRESENTATION* by which almost every kind of idea or experience, abstract or pictorial, is brought to life in sound.[6]

Perhaps you are familiar with these lines formulated by a committee of the Music Educators National Conference:

> Music speaks through a kind of common language which transcends some of the difficulties of the spoken word in communicating deep human feelings which are common to all men. It is able to transport us into the past, into different parts of the world, and into other seasons of the year. It can help us to understand the deep feelings of those who speak languages not commonly understood, to play, to work and to worship with those whose lives are lived under differing circumstances . . .[7]

---

[5] Howard Swan, unpublished letter to Gary Hall, August 27, 1975.
[6] *Ibid.*
[7] Ernst, Karl D. and Gary, Charles L., (eds.), *Music in General Education*. (Washington, D.C.: Music Educators National Conference, 1965), p. 3.

Why not make a beginning by creating your own definition of music? What does music mean to me? What is the source of its power? What are its functions?

147

As you interpret your philosophy of music in contacts with ACDA colleagues, try to do so as an optimistic realist. Pure optimism or pessimism have no place in a choral conductor's schedule. You remember this witty phrase of James Branch Cabell: "The optimist proclaims that we live in the best of all worlds and the pessimist fears that this is true." Why not be cognizant of that which is negative while stressing the positive aspects of any given situation? As a major part of your philosophy and procedure encourage the basic principle of quality in *all* music. There is certainly a place for entertainment music, but its materials and performances must be of the very best. Nor should there be a compromising of principles at any time or for any reason.

Do you know the excellent essay on "Quality in Music" which appears in the *Oxford Companion to Music*, edited by Percy Scholes? Let me read a few excerpts:

> As to the nature of "goodness" or "badness" in music . . . There have always been debates and probably always will be . . . There is no musical person of experience who does not assert the existence of grades of value in the musical repertory . . . The thoughtless division of music into "what I like" and "what I don't like" is too easy going. Music, like everything else, has its standards . . .

> The categories "good" and "bad" are altogether independent of the categories "complex" and simple; there is "good" simple music and "good" complex music, and "bad" simple and "bad" complex. Similarly, the categories of "good" and "bad" have no real connection with the categories of "classical" and "popular"; not only are there good symphonies and bad but there are good waltzes and bad.

What are the characteristics of "good" music?

> First, (says Scholes) good music has vitality and bad music often has not. It is easier to recognize this characteristic than to define it. A melody which wanders aimlessly is not vital. Compare with such a melody the opening phrase of anyone of Beethoven's sonatas, symphonies or string quartets—a phrase which in every instance arrests the attention . . . We feel ourselves at once to be in the presence of *life*. And in a "good" piece of music this feeling continues to the end of the composition.

> Orginality. We may say that good music is "individual" and "personal." Music lacking vitality is generally found to be a diluted extract of that of some other composer, or perhaps of so many other composers that no one composer can be named; or it may even be a thickened extract, for if there has been poured out upon the world much Mendelssohn and Water, there has equally been poured out much Mendelssohn and Glue . . .

Scholes continues his statement with a perceptive discussion of the qualitative traits of workmanship, proportion, and fitness, declaring, the element of personal taste, and as you would expect, the test of time. And he concludes in this fashion:

148

There is no acid test for "goodness" in music. The thoughful consideration of a trained taste must be applied, directed by some such method of analysis as that indicated above. It may not be possible by such means to prove a composition to be a masterpiece, but at all events great masses of second-rate music can thus be put aside.

Not all short-lived music is to be utterly condemned, for soundly-written journalism is a kind of literature. But it *must* be soundly written. There is, in fact, no excuse (beyond the commercial) for really "bad" music in any place or for any purpose.[8]

When a mutual and sympathetic understanding of the human spirit is built, people finally become persons.

A personal philosophy of choral music for self guidance, an optimistic spirit, an appreciation for that important element in music known as "quality"—What else may be needed in the making of a state president of the ACDA?

I believe that the enthusiasm with which most ACDA members regard their organization comes about because of their sense of pride in belonging to this group. I hope that you will see to it that this spirit is maintained and that it grows in its vitality and resource. How may this be done?

(1) Seize every way possible to communicate with the membership. Do so in a personal manner when it is possible to do so. Write, phone, create committees and attend their meetings so that you can know the participants.

(2) Print or write *names* whenever there is the opportunity.

(3) Thank people *always*, and find the personal way to do it.

(4) See that choral performances are listed in your state journals and attend some of them.

(5) Make the word "clinic" a verb rather than a noun. Ask a Texan!

(6) Encourage the exchange of musical ideas from place to place within your state as well as from state to state. Possible topics: All-State Choir organization, pros and cons of parent support groups, appointment of a committee to evaluate performance tapes or to answer questions on choral procedures through the columns of the state journal.

In your work for ACDA during this two year period all will learn much from practical experience about the do's and don't's of communication. I hope that eventually bridges can be built with other organizations with whom we should have more than a nodding acquaintance. I speak of the MENC, of the Society for the Encouragement of Barber Shop Singing, The National Association of Teachers of Singing, the groups primarily concerned with church music such as The American Guild of Organists, the several denominational associations, The Choristers Guild, etc.

---

[8] Scholes, Percy A., *The Oxford Companion to Music*, Seventh Edition. (London: Oxford University Press, 1947), pp. 770–773.

With thoughtful planning and plain hard work you can make it possible for many people to understand what it is that choral musicians are attempting to say and to do with their music. You have a magnificent opportunity to experience relationships. You will learn to sympathize with failure and rejoice with success. You will laugh with but not at others. When a mutual and sympathetic understanding of the human spirit is built, people finally become persons. And, you can make this happen if you desire to have it so!

At the conclusion of some remarks made on the occasion of his retirement dinner, the famous surgeon, Sir William Oster, made this revealing statement:

> I have three personal ideals. One, to do the day's work well and not to bother about tomorrow. The second ideal has been to act the Golden Rule as far as in me lay toward my professional brethren. . . . The third has been to cultivate such a measure of equanimity as would enable me to bear success with humility and the affection of my friends without pride. . . . [9]

When ACDA reaches the month of June, 1981 and you are required to relinquish your gavels, I trust that each one will have had the joy of realizing these three objectives.

---

[9] Beck, Emily M., (ed.), *Bartlett's Familiar Quotations*, Fourteenth Edition. (Boston, Little Brown and Co., 1968), p. 818.

Steps to Choral Excellence: Choices, Compromises and Decisions

The opening address at the 1980 Western Division convention of the American Choral Directors Association in San Diego, California.

Are the meanings of words as fascinating to you as they are to me? For example: at first glance the term "choice" seems to carry the same meaning as the word "decision." Yet as one thinks with the help of a dictionary, it appears that "choices" allow for options—the selection of alternatives—while decisions have to do with the arriving at final conclusions which are based upon thoughtful judgments. Choice carries an association with the tentative or temporary together with the implication of possible change. On the other hand, a decision comes about after several choices either have been made and then discarded, or have been found to be satisfying and self-serving. If we wish to gain *excellence* we make constant use of the principles of choice and compromise while moving steadily towards the happy state when decisions become final. Decisions testify to a maturity of judgment and even at times demonstrate the self-fulfillment of an individual.

Excellence . . . we might spend hours, even days in discussing whether there is in contemporary America a lack of desire to achieve high standards for performance. Has the motivation for doing something well disappeared in these troubled times? Is it possible to have a democratic society in which both equality and excellence exists? In spite of all that is happening to education, I believe that there are many choral musicians who do continue to be concerned about achieving excellence for themselves and for their students.

Now, what do we mean by "excellence"? The dictionary says "superiority" or "the condition of preeminence" or "to go beyond a limit or a standard."[1]

It seems that human beings always have been interested in the special quality of excellence. Syrus, who lived in the first century B.C., is credited with the pithy statement: "It takes a *long time* to bring

---

[1] "Editor and Publisher," as reported in the *Reader's Digest* December 1978, p. 27.

excellence to maturity."[2] Said the wise Aristotle, "With regard to excellence—it is not enough to *know*; we must try to have and use it."[3] James Bryant Conant, the respected President of Harvard University, told his graduating seniors some forty years ago that "each honest calling, each walk of life has its own elite, its own aristocracy based on excellence of performance."[4] And the twentieth century poet, Richard Wilbur, says it all in these brief lines:

> What is our praise or pride
> But to imagine excellence, and try to make it?
> What does it say over the door of Heaven
> But "homo fecit"?[5]

But, has the quest for excellence become almost an obsolete objective for musicians? Is there simply the doing of a job, the "going through the motions" form eight to four each day? Someone has said that a job holder is one who performs an assigned duty, usually in exchange for payment—while a true professional belongs to a group of *qualified* persons of one specific occupation. "Jobholders" or "professionals"—to which category do we belong?

All of us know many friends these days who have dropped by the wayside—disheartened, hurt, and defeated and sometimes quite angry with what happened to them, to their students, to music, to education, to society in general. It is wise then, at this particular moment, to consider standards, to speak of superior musicianship and excellence in teaching and performance?

This question has some potent answers furnished for us by John Gardiner. Many of you know that he has been a teacher, was affiliated with the United States Department of State, and for many years was President of the Carnegie Corporation and the Carnegie Foundation for the Advancement of Teaching. Perhaps he is known best as the founder of "Common Cause." Some years ago he authored a remarkable book which is pertinent to our discussion this morning. Its title—*Excellence*. Here are some excerpts from this thoughtful and helpful little volume:

> Some people may have greatness thrust upon them. Very few have excellence thrust upon them. They achieve it. They do not achieve it unwittingly by "doin' what comes naturally," and they don't stumble into it in the course of amusing themselves. All excellence involves discipline and tenacity of purpose.[6]
> Standards are contagious. They spread throughout an organization or a group cherishes high standards, the behavior of individuals

---

[2] Maxim 780, *Bartlett's Quotations*, p. 127.
[3] *Bartlett's Quotations*, p. 98—from Nichomachean Ethics, Chapter 9.
[4] Sermon: *"Our Fighting Faith," Bartlett's Quotations*, p. 1026.
[5] "For the New Railway Station in Rome" (1956) last stanza.
[6] Gardiner, John, *Excellence* (New York: Harper and Row, 1961).

who enter it is inevitably influenced. Similarly, if slovenliness infects a society, it is not easy for any member of that society to remain uninfluenced in his own behavior.[7]

(Motivation) More and more we are coming to see that high performance, particularly where children are concerned, takes place in a framework of expectation. If it is expected, it will often occur. If there are no expectations there will be little high performance.[8]

Education in the formal sense is only a part of society's larger task of abetting the individual's intellectual, emotional and moral growth. What we must search for is a conception of perpetual self-discovery, perpetual reshaping to realize one's best self, to be the person one could be. It includes not only the intellect but the emotions character and personality. It involves adaptability, creativeness and vitality. And it involves moral and spiritual growth.[9]

All of us probably will be in agreement with Mr. Gardiner when he asserts that "excellence is a curiously powerful word about which people feel strongly and deeply. But it is a word that means different things to different people. For as individuals contemplate the word 'excellence' they read into it their own aspirations, their conception of high standards and hopes for a better world."[10]

While at times it may be desirable to consider the topic of excellence as it applies to all segments of the choral art, this morning we will confine our discussion to only five areas out of which excellence may come: in musicianship, in the creation of one's philosophy of music education, in teaching, in performance techniques, in the choice of choral repertoire.

The dictionary gives us this terse statement concerning the meaning of *musicianship*. "Skill, taste and artistry in performing or composing music." Such would seem to require of the choral conductor a knowledge of many things. First, as Percy Scholes put it: "There must be an understanding of the physiology of voice, ear and hand; one needs also an appreciation of all examples of style and form—of theory and harmony."[11] There will be a knowledge of acoustics and a superiority with performance. To say it simply, excellence in musicianship for a choral conductor is based upon an ability to hear a score with one's eyes and ears and then to change into sound the printed page. These comments of Robert Shaw concerning musicianship are both pertinent and helpful:

(Beethoven's Ninth under Toscanini)

> *To say it simply, excellence in musicianship for a choral conductor is based upon an ability to hear a score with one's eyes and ears and then to change into sound the printed page.*

---

[7] *Ibid.*, p. 74.
[8] *Ibid.*, p. 101.
[9] *Ibid.*, p. 136
[10] *Ibid.*, p. xii (introduction).
[11] Scholes, Percy, *The Oxford Companion to Music*. (London: Oxford University Press, 1947). Articles on "Appreciation of Music" and "Form."

Toscanini's Beethoven was great not primarily because he could get more (from his performers) but because he could hear more (in the music) . . . There was over all his passion a mantle of sadness and defeat, as though (I think) he heard sounds and relations and forms in his own study which he could never actually achieve in performance.

That must have been very nearly my first consciousness of the conductor's art as synonymous with the art of hearing, of listening.[12]

(Re. a performance of *Singet dem Herrn*)

It is work of frightening difficulty. . . . And a couple of weeks prior to the concert we had rugged rhythm and a fair-to-middling sonority—but very little Bach. What we had was not a motet—but a contest.

Fortunately, we also had friends—among them musicians, and among the musicians Julius Herford. He attended a rehearsal, and after we had sung it through, I turned to him. "It seems to me," he said kindly "that if we all did a little less singing and a little more listening, we'd have more Bach."[13]

(Hindemith—*Requiem For Those We Love*)

And the thing that has been fresh and exciting to those who have been studying and rehearsing it has been the discovery of the vitality and spiritual eloquence of form itself. What we have faced—many of us for the first time—is the awareness that logic does not militate against the expressiveness of music. The fact that music is built with mind and craftsmanship and a sense of order . . . does not in any way decrease the degree of its "inspiration" or leave it emotionally sterile. For there is a spiritual quality to pattern itself, the awareness of which may be one of the chief qualifications of the mature artist.[14]

If musicianship involves the refinement of our ability to listen, it is to be hoped that any one of us could do a better job of hearing than that frustrated individual who after making a fortune decided to fulfill his life-long desire to conduct an orchestra. It seems that he hired one drummer, one saxophonist and thirty-three violinists. At the first rehearsal he conducted so poorly that the disgusted drummer asked the others to quit. They refused to do so because they were being well paid and besides, as one said, "the man surely must know something about music." When they began to rehearse again things were so terrible that the angry drummer started to beat his drums loudly and furiously. The conductor rapped for silence, glared at the musicians, and said, "Who did that?"[15]

If musicianship is concerned with the ability to hear and to understand the formal, how does one achieve excellence in formulating a philosophy for music education which can guide both teaching and

Whenever I'm called upon to talk to a group of young teachers who are just starting, I say, "One of the ways that you can tell you are proceeding toward maturity is whether you claim to know all the answers to all the questions that are asked of you." Most young teachers are afraid to say that they don't know. And yet what doctor knows all the answers? What lawyer knows all the answers? Why can't we say it? "I don't know that, but that is a very interesting question." Then don't say to the students, you go and find the answers, no you go and find the answer, if it's worthwhile, so that the next time you can say "Yes, I do know the answer to that one."—"Humanistic Education," Little Rock, 1979.

[12] Musselman, Joseph, *Dear People* (Bloomington, Indiana: University of Indiana, 1978), p. 63.

[13] *Ibid.*, pp. 63–64.

[14] *Ibid.*, p. 65.

[15] "Funny, Funny World" are reported in *The Reader's Digest*, December, 1978, p. 124.

performance? Such a credo must be both contemporary and practical. It should consider what choral music should accomplish for all who engage in music making in pre-school through adult life. It will be concerned with choices; choices of organizational procedures, responsible performance techniques, teaching methods, the knowledge of materials, and the disposition of one's time in working in all of these areas.

Here are three statements which might well be called philosophies of music education. One is by a fourth grade teacher. The second is excerpted from a dissertation written during the past year by the Educational Director of a Music Company. The last consists of several paragraphs taken from Bennet Reimers' *Philosophy of Education,* which I consider to be one of the most thoughtful books of this nature to be written in recent years.

> . . . left to its own devices, government and political funding, which first collects funds from us, then distributes them back, which necessitates costly administration, and which is dependent on election-conscious legislators—may provide us with programs which are wasteful, discriminatory, and ineffective imitations of the desired product. Madison Avenue (or Broadway?) techniques can be used to sell glittering and expensive music programs which, upon closer examination, will be found not to be pure gold. The temptation to substitute performances for comprehensive music programs exists, because public relations are important, and performances attract public support and funding. When these become ego trips for students, teachers, parents, and/or administrators, then students are being used, not educated.

> The implications of current research support the imperative that all students receive a quality, comprehensive education in the arts. Some of the most important of these implications for music educators are:
> (1) Music is needed by all children.
> (2) Music aids and enhances all learning.
> (3) The creativity developed through quality music programs carries over into life situations as "flexibility" and creative problem-solving ability.
> (4) The appreciation of one's own creative efforts (self-worth) leads to the appreciation of the efforts of others and the valuing of the cultural heritage we all share.
> (5) The participation in group art efforts, particularly music and dance, teaches the value of the individual in relation to the group, and develops social sensitivity and awareness.
> (6) Educational experiments in "arts-centered" schools have obtained evidence that a right-brain balanced education yields beneficial results in the mental-emotional-behavioral spheres which can be objectively measured in learning, creativity, motivation, and self-discipline.

> Our country's educational goals are for all citizens, guaranteed in the Constitution's "pursuit of happiness" phrase. Our government depends on an enlightened and educated electorate, as we are

allowed and expected to make decisions concerning the leadership and operation of the country. Our society cannot afford to offer less than a humanistic, whole-brained education to all citizens.[16]

In conclusion:

The music educator must adapt to a new and expanding role. In addition to demonstrating his skill as a teacher, he must become interpreter to the vast majority of parents, faculty, administrators and community members who still want and need an answer to the question, 'Why music education?'

One might think that music educators were the converted to whom preaching is unnecessary. If this were the case, there would be fewer unconverted board of education members. Unfortunately, more than half a century of traditional music education programs devoted to teaching the rudiments of the performance skills have not made the abandonment of these programs unthinkable. Music education as play, as entertainment, as therapy—these all have their merits and benefits; but the more these merits are relied on, the more the decision makers and the public are convinced that eliminating the music program, while regrettable, is no disaster. If music and arts specialists are willing to take responsible leadership roles for developing a total program of aesthetic education for the entire school population, this current crisis will be averted. If not. . . . [17]

Just as every other part of the curriculum has come under scrutiny in recent years, the performance program finds itself being examined according to changing conditions of education. . . . Old arguments stressing the value of performance no longer seem to make much impression and new arguments, reflecting altered conceptions of what constitutes high quality education, have not yet had time to be fully articulated. The need for serious thought about the function of performance in music education is most pressing.

This would not be the case if performance could continue to be regarded as either (1) special education for the musically talented or (2) an extra-curricular "activity" program on the level of special-interest clubs, social groups, etc. Neither of these alternatives is acceptable. . . . Neither contribution can serve to justify the existence of performance as a full-fledged curriculum subject, but each has values which should be recognized and supported as adjuncts to the main educational purpose of performance. . . .

Mastery of technique cannot by itself justify the enormous effort expended by so many children in learning to play or sing. Most children, by the nature of human talent and societal needs, will never progress beyond modest levels of technical prowess. After the initial excitement of getting involved and showing some progress. . . . the child often begins to realize that there are diminishing returns on his investment of time and energy (not to mention money). . . .

---

[16] Axup, Betty. "The Classroom to the Mainstream," *The California Music Educators Association News*, Nov. 1979, pp. 5–6.

[17] William, Raymond M. Excerpted from unpublished doctoral dissertation "Music Education in the State of California: Opportunity and Participation," *California Music Educators Association News*, Sept.-Oct., 1979, p. 5.

Musical mastery, whatever its limitations when considered as a separate entity, must remain of concern to the performance program because little can be achieved if technique does not constantly improve. A second factor must be added, however, which transforms technique from sterility to fruitfulness as a means of aesthetic education. This is the factor of musical understanding—the perception of and reaction to the expressiveness of music. This is the central goal of music education, to which performance must contribute if it is to be regarded as a central part of the enterprise. And the fact is that performance can contribute to musical understanding automatically. Musical understanding must be consciously, systematically, carefully *taught for.*[18]

Many times Reimer repeats his thesis that performance adds to the aesthetic experience only when it makes music more understandable to the performer. Now, we can agree that American choruses not only perform acceptably, but some of them also attain results which are amazingly close to perfection. But, how do their conductors work for excellence in areas of performance and music education?

First, there must be the definition and understanding of what I classify as the three choral "T's": Technique, Tone, and Tradition. In any musical score, which element is most important, and when and why does this happen? When choral techniques such as blend, proper intonation, choice of tempo, and all other similar factors present problems, how are such to be resolved? Secondly, what is the basic choral tone to be? Could it be described as "dark" or "bright"? Does its development lead to an "equal" or a "steeple" balance? Is a high degree of blend desirable, or does the director seek for more individuality by asking for increased vocal intensity? Finally, what are the formal or structural elements notated in each song which influence the relative importance of all other technical interpretive elements?

All of these aforementioned procedures must be successfully organized into the rehearsal periods if excellence in performance is to be realized. But, when and *how* do we rehearse what? How will the chorus and conductor know when a particular goal has been reached? More importantly, what means does the conductor utilize in communicating with the chorus? At times, drill is the only answer. But, what of all of the 'tions": explanation—inspiration—illustration—demonstration—comprehension? Can the conductor use these special idioms? The speaking voice must not be the sole means of communication. Look to the face, arm and body; be aware of the degree of intensity implied by the gesture. Plan for and encourage listening, questions, discussion, oral reporting, and vocal demonstration. Do not forget the periodic evaluation of progress made by the co-performers, the conductor and singers.

---

[18] Reimer, Bennet. *A Philosophy of Music Education* (Englewood Cliffs, New Jersey, Prentice-Hall, Inc., 1970), pp. 126, 128, 131, 132, 133.

Yet, while our singers perform well, all too frequently they are denied the opportunity to experience, to feel and to absorb the reality of music as a great and powerful art. It is wise occasionally to remind ourselves of the nature of the art which we serve. Three statements are helpful to me in this respect.

> *Music* as an art: the conscious production or arrangement of sounds or forms in a manner that affects the sense of beauty. It is intended to elicit an aesthetic response in a listener.

At Westridge School in 1986 where alumni, school trustees, and friends endowed a "Chair of Music" in Howard Swan's name. Dr. Swan taught at Westridge from 1938-1968.

158

Aesthetic: pertaining to a love for beauty. Pertaining to that which is tasteful.

Beauty (as in music): a pleasing quality associated with harmony or form, sound or color—with excellence of craftsmanship—truthfulness—originality—that rouses a strong contemplative delight.[19]

If choral music is to endow each participant with a sense of the beautiful, what is our first responsibility as conductors? Is not the answer found in the exploration of the harmonic, melodic, and other formal characteristics in the score, and the recognition by each singer that a voice can be used to express the qualities inherent in every individual personality? One finds musical beauty in structure, in ordered sound, in the pleasure which comes from the unanimity of attack and release, in the excitement of beat. Frequently there is the recreation in sound of a noble attempt by a gifted composer to say something significant. These are some of the ways which through rehearsal and performance music can become a necessary and vital educational experience.

Excellence as musician, philosopher, composer, performer, teacher—the very nature of excellence requires that great emphasis must be placed upon the choices and compromises of the choral conductor. Eventually, these lead to decisions which carry the inference of finality and which influence personal and professional goals. What are some of these choices faced by every conductor?

(1) How will we use our time and effort? In score study? Building the organization? personal involvement with the singers? choreography? improving our listening procedures? finding program materials?

(2) In how many ways can we communicate with our choirs? Which is our best procedure? pictorial speech? gesture? singing? use of piano? explanation? inspiration?

(3) What kind of choral tone? What of amplitude? registration? vocalization?
  a. Blend: to what degree—how much?
  b. Vibrato: Is a compromise necessary here? What is the effect upon the choice of repertoire?

(4) Authenticity of interpretation? How does our interpretive choice influence tone? tempi? ornamentation? importance of text?

(5) Involvement with administration and teachers and students? With departments of drama, journalism, printing, set construction, coaches?

(6) Area of specialization? How do you choose?

(7) Formation of answers to these questions: Why music? one's philosophy? place of public relations? entertainment? for the talented

---

[19] *The American Heritage Dictionary of the English Language* (Boston, Houghton, Mifflin Company, 1969).

One finds musical beauty in structure, in ordered sound, in the pleasure which comes from the unanimity of attack and release, in the excitement of beat.

ones? how much social implications? what of pops and musicals? for church musicians, the meaning of worship? Where does the musical growth of the individual belong in the picture? Where does the growth (and prestige) of the conductor fit into the picture?

Perhaps the most important decision to be made by choral conductors today is this: What materials, what kinds of repertoire should be sung by their choirs? Whether we classify program materials as a cause for or a result of other procedures or activities, the choice defines for all to see and hear our goals for our choirs. Shall music-making be for the purpose of entertainment, for public relations, as the means to win administration support, or as one way to explore the unique and powerful realities in aesthetic education? Curricula, choral organizations, rehearsal procedures, ideological beliefs, and school and church music calendars will be shaped by these choices. Make no mistake; either we opt for music which has popular appeal or we decide that music which has been considered great because of compositional genius and the test of time is the rightful heritage of our students.

This is not to say that there are no standards for the choice of materials or for the performance of pop music. There is music here which can be enjoyed as entertainment. But students will judge us as musicians by our selection of repertoire and the procedure by which it is rehearsed. They will talk among themselves concerning our response to music which consists only of a beat, to sounds which depend almost entirely upon movement for their expression, or the use of a text which either is sickeningly repetitive or frankly vulgar in its composition.

I ask myself many questions these days concerning the use of all types of pop music. Here are some of them:

(1) In order for music to be appreciated, must it be accompanied by movement? Is the joy of listening a forgotten activity?

(2) Do we possess and use any standards for the selection of texts? Incidentally, what have we done to the original meanings of the words "love" and "beauty"?

(3) Is the tentative and transient popularity of a composition with singers and audiences to be the sole test for its use?

(4) Is there a clash of styles in teaching the singing of "classical" and "pop" music? I refer to the treatment of consonants, certain pitch concepts, the openness of all vowel sounds, etc.

(5) Should we be encouraging all of our students to find a vocational outlet in commercial music?

(6) Can a choral group sing both styles of music equally well? If there are two ensembles, which group is "special?"

John Gardiner once asked a highly regarded music teacher what the secret was for his extraordinary success with students. This was

Why not believe in a creed which includes acceptance of new priorities? Will not such a statement suggest an honest cooperation with other areas of academic study; more attention given to elementary and junior high school music programs; an increased emphasis in rehearsals on matters of form and structure and all the elements of comprehensive musicianship; the asking for and receiving of opinions and help from our students?—"Symposium Summary, Observations and Reflections," *Southwestern Musician*, December 1977.

the reply: "First, I teach them that it is better do to it well than to do it badly. Many have never been taught the pleasure and pride in setting standards and then living up to them." And Gardiner's comment: "Standards! That is a word for every American to write on his bulletin board."[20]

Finally, some thirty-five years ago, Archibald T. Davison, a great teacher and conductor of the Harvard University Glee Club wrote these lines concerning music education in America:

> . . . the most serious demand (in America) is for teachers whose knowledge and experience of music is wide enough to guarantee a sound musical taste. Only when there is intelligent revolt against much educational material that now passes for music will there be hope for a productive music education in this country.[21]

I wonder what he would say about American choral music in 1982?

[20] *Bartlett's Quotations*, p. 98—from Nichomachean Ethics, Chapter 9.
[21] Apel, Willi, Editor. *Harvard Dictionary of Music* (Cambridge, Harvard University Press, 1947), p. 472.

5
Howard Swan:
The Historian

The Music of the Mormons, 1830–1865

The following excerpts exemplify Swan's love of history and his interest in the relationships between music and history. His thorough research reveals fascinating aspects of the early Mormons. The complete discourse was published in the May 1949 issue of The Huntington Library Quarterly *(Volume 12, Number 3).*

The music of the Church of Jesus Christ of Latter Day Saints is a vivid reflection of the story of the Mormon people. Hymn texts and melodies, the dance, songs of folk and composed origin, and choral and instrumental performance are forms of musical expression which record in unique fashion theological doctrine and the social and political life of the Saints. Wherever the Mormons have lived they have made music; any history of the church must include the story of its music.

The American frontiersman of the nineteenth century found the Saints a queer folk. For one thing, the Mormons believed in a "live" prophet, Joseph Smith, who claimed to receive advice in the form of heavenly revelations which solved for his people all problems of a spiritual and temporal nature. The church was governed by twelve apostles and by two orders of a reestablished Old Testament priesthood. The Mormons accepted the validity of miracles which might result from a laying on of hands, and it was whispered about on the frontier that some of the Saints even practiced polygamy . . .

After a thorough review of the historical aspects of the early years of the Mormons, Dr. Swan turns to the earliest examples of their music.

The importance of music in the new church was recognized by revelation imparted to Joseph Smith long before the migration to Utah. In July, 1830, Smith gave this divinely inspired intelligence to his wife Emma:

> And it shall be given thee, also, to make a selection of sacred hymns, as it shall be given thee, which is pleasing unto me, to be had in my church. For my soul delighteth in the song of the heart; yea, the song of the righteous is a prayer unto me, and it shall be answered with a blessing upon their heads.[1]

---

[1] Joseph Smith, *Doctrine and Covenants* (Salt Lake City, Utah, 1923), Section 25.

Emma Smith accordingly selected the songs for the first hymnal published by the church. The book, which appeared in 1835, contained ninety hymns. No tunes were printed in this first collection, since the church did not deem a psalmody essential until 1889, and thus many of the songs were sung to tunes already in favor with other religious denominations. Following a prevalent custom, word texts of familiar songs were altered to fit the peculiar theological requirements of the new faith.

Although Emma Smith and W. W. Phelps prepared a second edition of the hymnal in Nauvoo and invited others to join them in the task,[2] Mormon hymnody is indebted to the English edition of the hymnal for most of its content.[3] Four Mormon missionaries were sent to the British Isles in 1837, and by 1840 converts to the new faith had so increased in numbers that church authorities found it necessary to publish both a hymnal and a newspaper for use in the British mission.[4] The first issue of the newspaper *The Latter Day Saints Millenial Star* appeared in March, 1840, and the hymnal was published in July of the same year.[5] During the succeeding ten years nine editions of the hymnal, representing a total of approximately 54,000 copies, were printed in Europe, and reprints of the book were apparently supplied to the Saints in Utah in great numbers.[6]

The struggle between Mormons and Gentiles in Missouri and Illinois was pictured in songs strongly reminiscent of the stirring hymns of Martin Luther:

Come to me where there is no destruction or war.
Neither tyrants, nor mobbers, nor nations ajar;

---

[2] "Persons having hymns adapted to the worship of the Church of Jesus Christ of Latter Day Saints are requested to hand them, or send them to Emma Smith, immediately." *Times and Season*, Nauvoo, Illinois, Feb. 1, 1843.

[3] Wheelwright compared the index of Emma Smith's second hymnal of 1841 (304 hymns) and found that subsequent editions of the English hymnal used by the Saints in America reprinted but a third of this collection. Also, the influx of the British mormons to Utah tended to perpetuate the English editions. D. Sterling Wheelwright, "The Role of Hymnody in the Development of the Latter Day Saint Movement" (unpublished doctoral dissertation, University of Maryland, 1943), p. 73.

[4] The first British hymnal was edited by Apostles Brigham Young, John Taylor, and Parley P. Pratt. Young gave this explanation for publishing the book: "Concerning the hymn book, when we arrived here we found the brethren had laid by their old hymn books, and they wanted new ones; for the Bible religion, and all, is new to them. . . . " *Evening and Morning Star* (Kirtland, Ohio), I, 122.

[5] From an epistle of Joseph Smith, Jr. to the high council in England: "I have been favoured by receiving a Hymn Book from you, and as far as I have examined it, I highly approve of it, and think it to be a very valuable collection." *Millennial Star* (London, March, 1841).

[6] It is interesting to note that in 1871 the first book published in Utah Territory from movable type cast in the territory was the fourteenth edition of this hymnal. See Wheelwright, *op. cit.*, p. 78.

Where the system is perfect and happiness free;
And the life is eternal with God: Come to me.[7]

––––––––––––––––––

O! This is the land of the free!
And this is the home of the brave;
Where rulers and mobbers agree;
'Tis the home of the tyrant and slave.

Here liberty's poles pierce the sky
With her cap gaily hung on the vane;
The gods may its glories espy,
But poor mortals, its out of your ken.

The eagle soars proudly aloft,
And covers the land with her wings;
But oppression and bloodshed abound,
She can't deign to look down on such things.

All men are born equal and free,
And their rights all nations maintain;
But with millions it would not agree,
They were cradled and brought up in chains.[8]

In the following passages, Dr. Swan discusses instrumental music in Deseret and then the music of the early Mormon conventions.

The Mormon Church . . . was . . . enthusiastic in the endorsement of the joy to be found in music and in the dance. The church taught that if a Saint was to "live his religion" his life should be filled with a whole-hearted exuberance which would find expression in all forms of music. The Old Testament prophets had danced and had sung as a part of their praise to Jehovah. Latter Day Saints were advised to follow their example. Said President Young, "The world considers it very wicked for a Christian to hear music and to dance. Music belongs to heaven, to cheer God, angels and men. . . . Music and dancing are for the benefit of holy ones, and all those who do not worship God have no right to be there."[9]

Mormons had a particular regard for band music. Their first band had been organized from the ranks of the Nauvoo Legion of the Illinois Militia, and had led the Saints on their weary march to Winter Quarters. In 1850 the band was reorganized in Salt Lake City and gave regular con-

––––––––––––––––––

[7] *Fourteenth Edition of the Latter Day Saints Hymnal* (Salt Lake City, Utah, 1871), No. 283. Text by W. W. Phelps.

[8] Song by John Taylor, *Millenial Star* (London, Nov. 15, 1847). Tune, probably "Columbia, the Gem of the Ocean."

[9] Susa Y. Gates and Leah D. Widstoe, *The Life Story of Brigham Young* (New York, 1930), p. 263.

167

certs in the bowery.[10] The *Deseret News* for June 22, 1850, contained this complimentary statement:

> About one thousand people, citizens and strangers, attended the concert last Saturday evening; and so far as we are capable of judging, and have heard, all were not only satisfied but highly gratified; and will be ready for more at the proper time. The avails of the concert will be appropriated to defraying the expenses of constructing a carriage, for the use of the Band, while cheering the people. The carriage is rapidly progressing.

The band was a necessary adjunct for pioneer celebrations, for many dances, and was used even in services of worship. John Hyde, a Mormon apostate, in describing a meeting in the first Salt Lake Tabernacle spoke of "an instrumental band that plays marches, and even polkas, to enliven the feelings of the people, and get up the spirit."[11] William Chandless, who visited Salt Lake City in 1855, observed that the band "was called in upon all occasions of church and state; on cotillion nights a quadrille band, on Sundays a choir."[12]

The members of the Nauvoo Band were twenty-five in number, and instrumentation consisted of trumpets, trombones, clarinets, horns, cornets, and drums. The bandsmen were gaily attired in uniforms which consisted of "white dress coat and pantaloons, a sky blue sash, white muslin cravat and a straw hat for the covering of the head."[13]

While the Nauvoo Band gave its concerts and played for holiday celebrations during the summers, their services were also in great demand in the winter season as they furnish the music for numerous parties and balls. Christmas, New Year's Day, the opening of a new schoolhouse and the beginning of a session of the territorial legislature were occasions which always called for a dance. Gay social affairs often were sponsored by artisan groups: printers, carpenters, blacksmiths and masons. A typical dance entertainment was that which took place on Christmas Day, 1851. In attendance were those men engaged

---

[10] Until permanent buildings could be erected for pupuses of worship the Mormons used temporary quarters, or *boweries*. "Posts were set in the ground, and upon these rude pillars long poles were laid and securely fastened with wooden pegs or strips of rawhide. This framework, overlaid with timbers and brush, formed an umbrageous, if not a very substantial roof; a good shelter from the sun and fair though insufficient one from wind and rain. . . . At one end of these boweries it was customary to erect a platform and stand, well boarded in at the back, for the use of the presiding officers and speakers; a space in front being reserved for the choir. At first, seats would be improvized from whatever articles came handy, but in due time rude benches would follow, resting upon a floor or on the ground. . . . " From O. F. Whitney, *History of Utah*, quoted in *Heart Throbs of the West* (Salt Lake City, 1939), IV, 79.

[11] John Hyde, Jr., *Mormonism, Its Leaders and Designs* (New York, 1857), p. 39.

[12] William Chandless, *A Visit to Salt Lake* (London, 1857), p. 246.

[13] *Heart Throbs of the West* (Salt Lake City, 1939), IV, 120.

in the construction of the public buildings in Salt Lake City. The *Deseret News* reports this description of the party:

> Early on Christmas morning the brass band and several companies of serenaders with instruments made the rounds of the city. At ten A.M. the party began with thanksgiving and prayer—then the band struck up a tune and Governor Young and the Honorable H. C. Kimball and other distinguished personages lead off the first dance. We counted ninety-six to one hundred and forty-four persons in the hall at once. . . . The atmosphere of our hall was not polluted with tobacco fumes or the stench of the drunkard's breath: No! We breathed the pure mountain air, drank of the mountain stream and ate of the produce of the vallies. . . . About seven P.M. several individuals presented musical selections, followed by an address by Governor Young. The dancing and merriment continued to ten-thirty P.M.

At ten in the morning of the following day, the festivities commenced anew. During the day,

> The company was treated to a feast in the shape of a vocal and instrumental music by Mr. John Kay, his lady and two daughters, the one performed well on the guitar, and the other on the tambourine. . . . The dance continued till twelve P.M. when the assemblaged voiced their thanks to the managers and the party closed with the benediction.[14]

The church authorities did not countenance the dancing of polkas, waltzes, and the so-called "round dances." God fearing Saints were expected to derive their enjoyment from square and cotillion dances. One observer exclaimed, "They have even invented some new figures, among others a *double* quadrille in which each gentleman has two ladies, in fact, a *polygynic* quadrille."[15] All dances were opened and closed with prayer. At a legislative party in 1855 given by Governor Young in honor of Utah's territorial officers, the "quadrille band" was most elaborate and consisted of six first and second fiddles, a violoncello, double bass and flute.[16] In small settlements the merrymakers danced on a puncheon floor. Said one spectator, "Only one cotillion could be danced in such restricted quarters, while the waiting ones sat on trunks and benches eagerly awaiting their turn. . . . The music at these small family parties was usually two violins and sometimes an accordion or flute to accompany them."[17]

The bands also made a significant contribution to Mormon worship. John Gunnison, one of the first interested visitors to the valley, reported that "while the congregation is assembling and departing

---

[14] *Deseret News*, Jan. 24, 1852.

[15] Jules Remy and Julius Brenchley, *A Journey to Great Salt Lake City* (London, 1861), II, 181.

[16] *Deseret News*, Jan. 11, 1855.

[17] Susa Y. Gates and Leah D. Widstoe, *The Life Story of Brigham Young* (New York, 1930), p. 254.

from the house (of worship) it is usual for the large and excellent band of music to perform anthems, marches, and waltzes which drives away all sombre feelings and prepares the mind for the exciting and often eloquent discourses."[18]

While bands and choirs were given a prominent place in all Mormon meetings, their music was particularly significant in the general conferences of the entire church which were held in Salt Lake City each year during April and October. Every Saint who could make the proper arrangements attended "conference" and for a period of three days participated in a program which included the "sustaining" of church officials in their offices, and a balloting, always unanimous, on names of fallen Saints to be cut off from the church. A common observation of conference guests was that the Mormon congregation sang with virility and enthusiasm and that a varied repertoire was offered by the choir. John Hyde spoke of the choir singing "from original Mormon songs in the tune of 'Old Dan Tucker,' to Bach's chants and Handel's oratorios."[19] Remy and Brenchley, who visited Salt Lake City in 1855, reported, probably with some exaggeration, "The Mormons have a feeling for sacred music; their women sing with soul, and the execution is in no notable degree surpassed by that which is heard either under the roof of Westminster, or in the frescoes of the Sistine Chapel."[20] Another visitor wrote of the Welsh choir which "exhilarates all present by singing one of their hymns to one of their churning, wild, romantic airs."[21]

During the first years of its service the Salt Lake City tabernacle choir probably sang with greater enthusiasm than artistic finesse. Direction of the group usually was given over to an individual of Welsh or English descent who possessed only an elementary understanding of choral techniques. Nevertheless, John Parry, the first conductor of the choir, insisted that his singers memorize the words and music of their songs, and he searched the settlements in order to secure hymns and music books for his choir.[22]

An excellent sample of the choral literature sung by early Mormon choirs is found recorded in the minutes of the General Conference of the Church of Jesus Christ of Latter Day Saints which met in April, 1852:[23]

[18] John W. Gunnison, *The Mormons or Latter Day Saints in the Valley of the Great Salt Lake* (Philadelphia, 1852), p. 37.

[19] John Hyde, *op. cit.*, p. 39.

[20] Remy and Brenchley, *op. cit.*, II, 56.

[21] Gunnison, *op. cit.*, p. 37.

[22] Letter of Joseph Hyrum Parry to the editor of *Druid*, Pittsburgh, Pa., Jan. 1, 1938, p. 6. Reprinted in *Utah Genealogical and Historical Magazine* (Salt Lake City), XXIX, 63.

[23] *Deseret News*, Apr. 17, 1852.

"Lord, In the Morning, Thou Shalt Hear"—210th hymn sung by the choir, directed by James Smithies, chorister.

"The Morning Breaks, The Shadows Flee"—Choir.[24]

"In Deseret We're Free"—Solo by John Kay, written by W. W. Phelps.

"Before Jehovah's Awful "rone"—Choir.[25]

"The Spirit of God Like a Fire is Burning"[26]

"The Seer"—solo by John Kay.[27]

"The Son of God Will Come"—Hymn written by Eliza R. Snow.[28]

Reporting on a subsequent conference meeting in October, 1852, the *Deseret News* observed that "the choir *chaunted* a piece of sacred music,"[29] and again "the choir sung a hymn, when the double bass viol was brought into use for the first time in this place."[30] A selection sung for the April, 1853, Conference, was Handel's "Hallelujah," probably done with melodeon accompaniment.[31]

Not all the Saints were enthusiastic in praise of the quality of choral music which they heard at conferences. Jonathan Grimshaw, a self-appointed critic, delivered himself of several bristling comments in a communication to the editor of the *Deseret News*. Grimshaw said, in effect:

1. Why do not the people of this territory like choruses, quartets, etc.? Because they cannot understand the words when many are singing at the same time.

2. I hope that soon, books of words will be printed or made available for each concert.

3. In the meantime, the hymn should be given out from the stand so that the people could follow that which is to be sung in their hymn books.[32]

This article includes descriptions of numerous historical events, brought to life by musical examples. The following is Dr. Swan's conclusion.

It is related of Brigham Young that he exclaimed as he first looked out over the valley of the Great Salt Lake: "This is the place!" If Father Brigham were alive today he would see much in this same valley to give him concern. He would deplore the number of Gentiles who call Utah their home, whose ancestors came to secure the metals which Brigham

---

[24] The missionary hymn written by P. P. Pratt and printed by him on the cover of the first issue of the London *Millenial Star* in 1840.

[25] Text by Isaac Watts.

[26] *Latter Day Saints Hymnal*, Edition of 1927, No. 127.

[27] *Latter Day Saints Hymnal*, Edition of 1927, No. 96.

[28] Written by Eliza R. Snow, a contemporary Utah poetess, best known for her authorship of a favorite Mormon hymn, "O My Father."

[29] Oct. 30, 1852.

[30] Oct. 16, 1852.

[31] *Deseret News*, Apr. 16, 1853.

[32] *Deseret News*, Feb. 2, 1854.

Young despised—copper and silver and gold. He might resign himself to the conviction that Salt Lake, once a fueling station for immigrants bound for California, now acts in the same capacity for giant airliners. If his sermons were shouted today from the tabernacle pulpit, President Young's admonitions might be questioned before they were obeyed. But Brigham Young would find many Saints who were living their religion in the old way, with a homely kind of industry and neighborliness which is respected throughout the West. He would dance and sing with a people who continue to believe that most forms of pleasure are "holy unto the Lord." He would share with his brethren a deep affection for the mountain home to which he had led their forefathers, a love for Deseret which finds expression in the words of the old hymn which he knew so well:

O ye mountains high, where the clear blue sky
Arches over the vales of the free,
Where the pure breezes blow and the clear streams flow
How I've longed to your bosom to flee.
O Zion! dear Zion! land of the free,
Now my own mountain home, unto thee I have come.
All my fond hopes are centered in thee.[33]

---

[33] *Latter Day Saints Hymnal*, Edition of 1927, No. 337. Text by Charles W. Penrose, tune, "Lily Dale."

The First American Performance of *La Boheme*

Swan wrote this piece in 1951 to accompany No. 14 of a series of facsimiles of early western theatre programs issued to members of The Book Club of California.

Casual indeed was the decision which brought to Los Angeles the honor of hearing the first performance in the United States of Puccini's opera, *La Bohéme*. Flushed by the success of a series of operatic presentations in South America and Mexico, the Del Conte Italian Opera Company of Milan decided to enter the United States by way of the southwest in order to hurry to San Francisco, a city whose inhabitants had been enthusiastic about grand opera for nearly half a century. Before they left Mexico City, however, the company manager received a pleading letter from Los Angeles asking that the singers stop for a week and present their interesting repertoire in that city. Since there was ample time for both engagements, the request was granted and thus, by chance, Los Angeles heard three performances of *La Bohéme* before it was sung in San Francisco, New Orleans, Philadelphia, or New York.

The request for a Los Angeles engagement had been written by Charles Modini-Wood, whose passion for grand opera perhaps influenced his better judgment, for he knew that Los Angeles never had been particularly receptive to music drama. For several years Wood had studied in Italy and then had concertized in many parts of the world. After travelling to Southern California for the sake of his health the tenor had met in Los Angeles a young soprano, Mamie Perry, who had had a short operatic career of her own in Europe. Soon the two singers were married and happily renounced their own operatic ambitions to sing for an occasional local charity. Mrs. Wood's father, W. H. Perry, then purchased the "new" Los Angeles Theater and installed Wood as its lessee-manager. With such a personal music history, little wonder that the singer-entrepreneur could not allow an operatic organization to come within 500 miles of Los Angeles without booking the group for an appearance in his theater.

From the very first the engagement of the Del Conte company seemed doomed to failure. Grand opera could not interest a people who were talking feverishly in terms of the new oil strikes on the outskirts of the city, or of the rapid development of southern California's electric railways and the hydro-electric power to run them brought from swift mountain streams. The fight for a free harbor at San Pedro was an even more absorbing topic of conversation. Furthermore, when a tired business executive wanted recreation he gave but little thought to music. Instead, his time was devoted to the exciting game of golf which he could play on the new course way out on Western Avenue. His wife was busy with her many invitations to afternoon teas and musicales—society and opera were not yet the inseparable companions of a later day.

Also, no one knew much concerning the company that manager Modini-Wood was bringing to the city. Musicians would have preferred hearing a greater number of familiar operas rather than *Otello, Un Ballo In Maschera,* and *La Bohéme*—all new to Los Angeles. Nor did the advertisements dispel public apathy concerning the engagement. Communication with the press agent for the company evidently did not exist, for the newspapers carried no notices about the organization until a scant three days before the first performance and even then, the public was given no information about singers who would appear. Of course, the *Herald* informed its readers that " . . . *La Bohéme* was *not* the same opera as *The Bohemian Girl* . . . " and the *Times* spoke glowingly of " . . . the 91 people in the company . . . " and the " . . . 36 Professors from Mexico City who played in the orchestra. . . . " Strangely enough, the orchestra was reduced to 19 instrumentalists by the time that the engagement opened.

The Italians were supposed to sing first in the city on October 11, but a railroad washout in Arizona delayed for one day their arrival in Los Angeles. Furthermore, heavy downpours of rain, "most unusual" for the season, plagued the company during their entire engagement. However, newspaper accounts agree that the singers "though not beautiful," were in excellent voice, and that the orchestra was quite the best supporting instrument heard since the appearance of Theodore Thomas' National Company ten years before.

But what of the success of *La Bohéme*? Only 532 persons in Los Angeles cared enough to hear the first United States performance of what has become one of the most popular of American operas. The company received but $327.70 in receipts for its efforts of the evening. While the *Herald* reported that " . . . the spontaneous outburst of enthusiasm at the end of the third act has never been surpassed in the city . . . " the same newspaper noted sadly that " . . . the opera did not attract the people of wealth. Italian and Mexican citizens were conspicuous in the audience, but the bon-ton of American society sought its

174

pleasure elsewhere. . . . The great majority are not attracted unless the music is fairly familiar to them. . . . "

Thus the bit of musical fame which had come by accident to Los Angeles found most of her citizens not only uninformed, but completely uninterested.

Number Eight

PIONEER WESTERN PLAYBILLS

The first American performance of

LA BOHEME

at the "New" Los Angeles Theater

Los Angeles, October, 1897

COMMENTARY BY HOWARD SWAN

LOS ANGELES THEATRE

H. O. WYATT, MANAGER.

PROGRAMME

Thursday Evening and Saturday Matinee,
First time in this city of the Sublime Opera in Four Acts, by
G. Puccini, words by G. Giacosa and L. Illic.

LA BOHEME

CAST.

Rudolfo, poet... ... ...Signor Giuseppe Agostini
Schaunard, musician...................Signor Luigi Francesconi
Benoit, inn keeper......................Signor Antonio Fumagali
Mimi............................Senorita Linda Montanari
Marcello, painter ....Signor Cesare Cioni
Coleine, philosopher ....Signor Victorio Girardi
Alcidoro, counsel of estates.........Signor Antonio Fumigali
Musetta............................Senorita Cleopatra Vicini
Parpignol...........................Signor Aristide Masiero
Sergeant-at-Arms.....................Pedro Lopez
Students, Bergers, Commercial Merhants, Modistes, Venders,
Soldiers, Singers, Waiters, etc., e.c.
Scene—Paris, France.   Time—A. D. 1830.

ACT I.—Attic, top floor Latin Quarter.
ACT II.—In the Latin Quarter.
ACT III.—The Boulevarde and Gate of d'Enfer.
ACT IV.—Attic on top floor in Latin Quarter.

Friday Evening—*Verdi* ....Ernani
Saturday Evening—*Verdi*....................Il Trovatore

STAFF.

Signor Alfonzo Del Conte......... ....Director
Mr. Al. Harris..Manager
Signor Palocio...Treasurer
Mr. Ed. Hageard ....General Agent
Signor Ettore Drog..............................Stage Manager

The Great Saloma Quartette appears in the Orchestra.
Signor Pietro Valini ....Leader of Orchestra
Luis E. Saloma ....Violin Concertante

NEXT WEEK Monday, Tuesday and Wednesday

Italian Grand Opera Co.

IN REPERTOIRE

The Santa Monica and Pasadena Electric Cars for Colegrove,
Pasadena and Santa Monica wait un il after the play.

A Listener's Report on European Music: Implications for Americans

Awarded a Ford Foundation Grant in the spring of 1963, Dr. and Mrs. Swan traveled four and one-half months in nine European countries studying the "music-making" of many eminent conductors and performing ensembles. This report shares his impressions.

In the spring and summer of 1963 I traveled four and one-half months in nine European countries. A Ford Foundation Fellowship made it possible for me to attend many rehearsals—to hear a great number of concents—and most important—to talk with music educators, musicologists and performers.

Before I speak of certain experiences and impressions it should be made perfectly clear that these are admittedly subjective in nature. All of us are acquainted with the kind of person who is fully prepared to write a book on the political, social, and economic picture of any country after he has visited in its capital city for a total of three days! In other words—I do *not* consider myself an "authority." On the other hand, I saw and heard some things that were interesting to me—and I trust that they will be the same for you.

First—I was surprised to hear from conductors in Austria, France and Germany that they considered that music in the United States in its total effect was superior to that produced in their own countries. (And this from those states that produced a Mozart, Bach, Beethoven, Brahms, Wagner, Schubert, and many other composers!) Musical authorities gave three reasons for their belief. One—in the United States—the professional artist, particularly in his earlier years performs with an amateur chorus or orchestra. In our country, they said, the soloist will never debase himself nor his profession by appearing as a member of such an organization. This means that with a few exceptions we do not have strong amateur groups. "Furthermore—in the United States, you have many fine professional orchestras of first rate caliber. In this country there are only two or three such even though the organizations are subsidized in part by the state." A third statement—repeated to me in Austria and Germany was sobering in its impact. "Between 1930–1940 we Germans and Austrians drove our finest musicians, teachers, performers, and scholars out of the country. So many of us who are teaching now were trained in a haphazard fashion under second rate teachers. Our very best people went to America. We are now harvesting that which we sowed thirty years ago."

Second, I learned that there is an apparent division among European musicians which is determined by the nature of their responsibilities. The church musician (who, incidentally, usually has been trained in a different institution from that attended by the music educator) knows very little about the school choral situation in his community—and the director of the professional group has absolutely no contact with other musicians except for those enrolled in his own organization.

Third, although such a sweeping statement is dangerous to make, it appears that European musicians at all levels of activity—and this includes the amateurs—are better scholars, better *students* of music than we in America.

Fourth, although the world has grown smaller in many ways, it is unfortunate that barriers of ignorance and poor communication keep the musicians of one country from knowing much about music which is being produced in another part of the world. When the Viennese choirs sing contemporary compositions, they are written by Austrian composers. English choirs perform English music, and the same practice prevails in Germany, Denmark, and France. I asked many men if they knew the music of our American composers. One conductor was familiar with Copland's mane—the others were unable to speak knowingly of any American. At the biennial meeting of the German Music Educators' Association in Stuttgart, many of the choruses and orchestras sang and played compositions of Karl Marx (NOT the Communist philosopher!) Yet, in Vienna, a city less than 300 miles distant from Stuttgart, they had never heard of the man. Do any of us use his compositions? Do we perform the works of Germans: Pepping and Karl Meister, the Austrians: Cerba and Heiler, the Englishmen: Ian Hamilton and MacMillan, and the Swedes: Wikander and Lidholm? It is sad that only the "experimental" composers seem to be known outside their native countries.

Fifth, European audiences listen to music with tremendous concentration. They are so very quiet that the stillness almost bursts one's ears.

I was privileged to attend several days of meetings of the German Music Educators Association which took place in Stuttgart. This conference would correspond to a national gathering of the MENC in our

Because of TV's popularity will music in time become something to be watched rather than listened to? Instead of an activity in which we all can participate will music soon be a spectator sport? Can a few concerts for children at the Music Pavilion in Los Angeles provide a satisfactory substitute for the hundreds of elementary schools in California where no music is heard?— **"A Question of Balance," Occidental College, 1986.**

own country. The first thing that I noticed was that in strolling about the exhibits, while there were musical scores in abundance, recordings, and textbooks, there were no instruments to be seen except for a few recorders and one cello. When I asked about this, I was told that those in charge of German schools have no money with which to purchase instruments. Furthermore, the only instrumental organizations which played during the course of the convention—and they were principally groups made up of string players (no bands)—came from private or independent schools.

Yet, before we draw any hasty conclusions may I report that: 1) many of the teachers stood for more than an hour to listen to a scholarly lecture on music history; 2) you could not secure a ticket for an evenings operatic performance which was the first presentation of a new German work; 3) I sat through a remarkable performance presented by a chorus of one hundred seventy-five junior and senior high school singers accompanied by a professional orchestra. There were approximately 3500 in the audience. The program: first half, Bach "Magnificat"; second half, Mozart "Requiem." When some of the audience began to applaud as the chorus and soloists and orchestra moved out onto the stage, others hissed as if to say "This kind of music is best listened to in complete silence." And when I went backstage to offer my congratulations to the conductor in the usual American fashion, I found that his door was locked even though I knew that he was in the room. Apparently, he felt that it was Bach and Mozart who should be applauded and not himself.

Finally, when I asked one world famous conductor if he would be willing to answer a few questions related to matters of interpretation, he exploded with these words, "Ah, you Americans! You always wish to be told exactly on what page of what book you may find the answer to the problem which is bothering you. You rush to a teacher and expect him to explain in a few minutes' time how one may understand any musical score. . . . I admire your eagerness, but when are you going to learn that it takes a lifetime of study to become a real musician? Why don't you learn to find your own answers?"

My first reaction was one of dismay and even anger. Then I began to wonder if he was right about us.

Now, of course I could speak of the great interest that Europeans have in contemporary music—the numbers of young Americans that are singing in their opera houses—their love for music and art and fine literature. I could tell of their technical know-how when it comes to staging opera. European musicians are very proud of their profession—it is truly a "calling" as far as they are concerned.

What are the implications of all of this for you and for me?

(1) To some degree we have forgotten the power that is in music. Over the centuries music making has changed but music *has not*. If our

> *We need to know better how to study a score—how to bring to life the composer's ideas as he has set them down in the score in the form of musical symbols.*

181

times call for new ways of doing the job, then let us find these ways, but let us never forget that we have the privilege of serving an art which continues to mean much to many people.

(2) We music educators have at times been mistaken in some of our emphases during the past two or three decades. All of us wish to discharge properly our responsibilities. Yet, I wonder if this has not meant for many of us a *mastery of technique* rather than a master of the score? We need to know better how to study a score—how to bring to life the composer's ideas as he has set them down in the score in the form of musical symbols. We need to do much more listening, to read what composers have said concerning their own work, to rebuild our minds and ears and that quality which we call "good taste." In Europe, I saw no evidence that showmanship ever was considered as a substitute for musical integrity.

(3) I am going to do everything in my power to advance the cause of American music, and I invite you to do the same.

(4) Time and again as I traveled about, I saw and heard so much being done with so little in the way of resources. I wonder if we music educators these days do not indulge in a kind of self-pity—at times we are very sorry for ourselves. You know the story—What can I do with a six period day? My principal doesn't think much of music—I don't have a decent place in which to rehearse. . . . There are too many college preparatory subjects in the curriculum; music doesn't have a chance. . . . They won't let me buy another sousaphone this year. . . . Tenors don't exist anymore. . . . What chance has music with the present emphasis on science? etc., etc., and, we end our complaints by wistfully asking:

When, oh, when will the pendulum begin its swing the other way? When will the arts and the humanities come into their own? When will they occupy the place of importance which was theirs fifteen to twenty years ago?

And I ask of you as I ask of myself—when are *we* going to start pushing the pendulum? What are we waiting for?

I saw so many examples of the truth that music speaks powerfully to all kinds of people. I believe that it can and does do the same here in America. I am certain that each of us in his own school or college can find the way to make things go properly, powerfully, magnificently, perhaps not by using the methods and the forms that we enjoy, but by seeking out others which *fit* in our own particular situation.

Los Angeles: American City

In this article, Swan describes the history of music in Los Angeles from the time of its settlement in 1781 to the present. The piece was prepared for inclusion in The New Grove's Dictionary of Music and Musicians, published by Macmillan, London, 1980.

A company of Spanish soldiers, priests and immigrants established a settlement in 1781. For nearly a century the only formal music to be heard in the city and its environs was provided by choirs of Indians attached to the Franciscan missions or by amateurs who gathered to perform for some significant occasion. The population grew after the completion of railway lines in 1885, as did its appreciation of cultural values. Between 1880 and 1890 the first real theatres were built; several universities and colleges were founded, and professional musical organizations were begun. By 1915 Los Angeles had its own symphony orchestra and supported several concert series. The Metropolitan, Chicago, and San Carol Opera companies made occasional visits, and a periodical, the *Pacific Coast Musician*, was published in the city.

The city's temperate climate was responsible for the arrival of the first film companies in 1913. Although instrumentalists were needed to play background music for the silent films, the introduction of sound films in 1927 created a far greater demand for musicians of every kind. Each studio employed an orchestra of symphonic proportions, providing a vast pool of musical talent which helped to make Los Angeles a center for radio, television and the recording industry. In 1950 television first made use of, then quickly abandoned most forms of musical expression, together with the increased production of films in Europe. This created difficulties for many Los Angeles musicians from 1960 onwards.

Los Angeles did not acquire an adequate concert hall until relatively late in its history. Hazard's Pavilion, first opened in 1887, was a crude wooden structure in which musical presentations alternated with boxing matches and flower festivals. The Temple, later the Philharmonic Auditorium, was built as a church in 1907; musical activity in the hall was limited by the needs of church authorities for nearly 60 years. The massive Shrine Auditorium constructed in 1927 was only partly satisfactory for opera. However, in 1964 a group of citizens led by Dorothy Buffum Chandler was responsible for the financing and construction of three theatres in a Music Center complex in central Los

Angeles. The Dorothy Chandler Pavilion (capacity 3250) is adequate for almost all types of concert presentation; the Ahmanson Theater (capacity 2100) is used for light opera productions; and the Mark Taper Forum (capacity 750) for recitals of chamber music.

The erection of the Music Center was a great stimulus to musical activity in Los Angeles. Six local organizations were authorized to use the theatres and became resident musical groups of the Center: the Southern California Symphony—Hollywood Bowl Association, sponsor of the Los Angeles PO; the Los Angeles Civic Light Opera Association; the Center Theater Group; the Southern California Choral Music Association; the Music Center Opera Association; and the Young Musicians Foundation. The last-named organization holds auditions designed to award career grants to young musicians; it also sponsors the Début Orchestra, composed of carefully selected young instrumentalists aspiring to professional careers who play an annual series of concerts in the Pavilion.

After several unsuccessful attempts to form a professional orchestra, the Los Angeles SO was founded in 1898 and began an annual series of concerts with Harley Hamilton as conductor. In 1919 the organization became the Los Angeles PO and until 1934 received financial support from William A. Clark Jr. In addition to its programmes in the Music Center and the Hollywood Bowl, the orchestra often plays in the city's environs. It has toured Europe (1967, 1973), Japan (1969, 1972) and elsewhere in Asia (1967). Its conductors have included Walter Rothwell (1919–28), Georg Schnéevoigt (1928–9), Artur Rodzinski (1929–33), Otto Klemperer (1933–43), Alfred Wallenstein (1943–56), Eduard van Beinum (1956–8) and Zubin Mehta (1962–). Partly because of the suburban character of the region, about 20 semi-professional orchestras exist within a radius of 60 miles from the centre of Los Angeles. The best known are in Glendale, Long Beach and Pasadena.

The Coleman Chamber Music Association of Pasadena presented the first of an annual series of concerts in 1904. Other programmes of chamber music are sponsored by the Monday Evening Concerts in the Art Museum, the Music Guild, and the Los Angeles Chamber Music Association.

Much music in Los Angeles is presented out of doors. The Hollywood Bowl concerts were established in 1922 with Alfred Hertz as conductor. In a natural amphitheater formed by the hills bordering Hollywood, the Bowl property was purchased by popular subscription in 1924 and presented to the County of Los Angeles. The early programmes consisted of symphonic and choral concerts together with ballet and opera presentations. Later seasons have followed a pattern of an eight-week summer series offering concerts of serious and lighter music. The Hollywood Bowl Orchestra and Los Angeles SO now have

How can I forget the time at Meadowbrook (Michigan) when, after expressing his concern that the choir of 160 community college singers were not motivated properly to sing the **B minor Mass,** *[Robert Shaw] proceeded to have them dance as they sang the work without a pause. "Now, move the way that the music makes you feel," was his explanatory statement. And, after they had utilized almost every dance step known to man and lay exhausted on the floor, he commented: "Now, that is the way that you must feel and project at tomorrow's performance," and he walked quickly from the room. Needless to say, the concert was a magnificent emotional repeat of that which had happened on the previous day.—"Recollections,"* The Choral Journal, **April 1986.**

the same members and management. In spite of changes in musical policy and financial difficulties, parking problems and aircraft noise, the concerts are now patronized by a large public. Other southern California 'bowls' are in the suburban cities of Redlands, Burbank, Ojai and Laguna Beach.

Although a troupe from Mexico presented the first North American performance of *La bohème* in Los Angeles in 1897, the city has not been able to establish its own opera. The Lyric Company of Chicago made the first of several visits in 1913, the San Francisco Opera visited annually from 1937 to 1969, and the New York City Opera Company began annual vistis in 1967. Although the Civic Opera Association hopes to form a resident company in Los Angeles, its activities in the early 1970s were confined to helping to sponsor productions by visiting organizations.

Los Angeles has always enjoyed and supported choral music. The Ellis Orpheus and Lyric choral societies began in 1888 and are still active. Many schools, colleges and churches have excellent choral programmes; there are also several semi-professional choruses in the region. The Roger Wagner Chorale (of 100 singers conducted by Roger Wagner) is the only professional resident chorus in the country with its own season. The Southern California Vocal Association, composed of music teachers, sponsors choral festivals in which more than 40,000 children participate each year.

Although Stravinsky lived in the area and Schoenberg taught in Los Angeles, their musical influence on the community was slight. Interest in music is primarily stimilated by the activity at the Music Center, by the broadcasts of radio station KFAC, by the cogent musical reporting of the *Los Angeles Times* and by an unusual amount of composition and performance which takes place at the many colleges and universities in the area.

The two most important music instruction centres in Los Angeles are the School of Music in the endowed (private) University of Southern California (USC) and the Music Department of the (state) University of California at Los Angeles (UCLA). USC, founded in 1880, began to offer music instruction in 1884 and the school of music was formally established in 1892. In the 1970s the school had about 700 students and 90 instructors, offering BM, AB, MM, AM, DMA and PhD degress in performance, music education, choral music, church music, theory, composition and musicology. UCLA was established in 1882 as the Los Angeles State Normal School and became the southern branch of the University of California in 1919, instituting a music syllabus in 1939. In the 1970s the department had about 350 undergraduate and 100 graduate students, and 65 instructors, offering BA, MA, MFA and PhD degrees in musicology, ethnomusicology, music education, composition and performance practice. An important Insti-

185

tute of Ethnomusicology, founded in 1961 by its director, Mantle Hood, was absorbed into the Music Department in 1974. There is also musical activity at the California Institute of the Arts, which began as the Los Angeles Conservatory of Music in 1884.

In 1974 USC and UCLA joined with several other Los Angeles educational institutions to establish the Arnold Schoenberg Institute, which will contain virtually all Schoenberg's literary and musical manuscripts, as well as his library and other items from his studio. Five libraries in the Los Angeles metropolitan area have extensive music holdings: the Los Angeles Public Library, the libraries of the universities of California (including rare early Venetian opera librettos, the Meredith Wilson Library of American popular music, and film scores) and Southern California (including a unique collection of Russian operas, 18th-century *opèras comiques* and cinema and television music), the William A. Clark Memorial Library and the Henry E. Huntington Library in San Marino.

BIBLIOGRAPHY

C. E. Smith: *The Philharmonic Orchestra of Los Angeles* (Los Angeles, 1930).

I. M. Jones: *Hollywood Bowl* (New York, 1936).

O. F. da Silva: *Mission Music of California* (Los Angeles, 1941).

L. Jacobs: *The Rise of the American Film* (New York, 1944).

C. McWilliams: *Southern California Country* (New York, 1946).

R. D. Saunders, ed.: *Music and Dance in California and the West* (Hollywood, 1948).

A. Goldberg: 'Los Angeles', *Musical USA* (New York, 1949).

H. Swan: *Music in the Southwest* (San Marino, 1952).

N. Shavin: 'Music, Television's Stepchild', *Musical Journal*, xv (1957), 12, 24.

P. Yates: 'Los Angeles, the Demi-Wasteland: Music in Southern California', *High Fidelity*, xii (1962), 38, 110.

A. Goldberg and others: 'The Music Center', *Los Angeles Times* (6 Dec 1964).

J. Meggett and R. Moritz: 'The Schoenberg Legacy', *Notes*, xxxi (1974–5), 30.

Music Teaching in
Southern California
100 Years Ago

This recent talk was presented to the Los Angeles Chapter of the National Association of Teachers of Singing.

For a few minutes I invite you to look with me at the southern California of 100 years ago. What was happening to music in this part of the world in the years 1860-1875?

Southern California in the eighteen-fifties and sixties was anything but a Paradise. The manners and the morals of the people were definitely Latin-American; you will recall that the territory had been ceded to the United States government only a dozen years before the time of which we are speaking. The Gold Rush had come and gone, and much of the criminal element which always is a part of such a violent, exciting event had drifted down to this part of the State. Murders, robberies, lynching and crimes of every nature were common occurrences. Listen to a description of Los Angeles and our fair southland as it was made by a visitor in the fifties:

> The city the Spaniards have christened, I know not why, "The Angels," has nothing angelic about it, far from it; and really I do not see how any person, with the best desire in the world, can find anything remarkable in it. Irregular and ill built, it has a dirty aspect. The greater part of the houses, of Mexican construction, are built with adobes, only one story high, with flat roofs, covered, instead of tiles, with a coat of bitumen obtained from a spring near the city. By the side of these filthy and miserable dwellings, the foreigners, drawn to California by the discovery of gold, have built houses much more comfortable, elegant, and better built.[1]

William H. Brewer, engaged in a geological survey of California, wrote to his brother in 1860: "We all continually wear arms—each wears a bowie knife and pistol while we have always for game or otherwise a Sharp's rifle, Sharp's carbine, and two double barrel shot-

---

[1] Remy, Jules and Brenchley, Julius, *A Journey To Great Salt Lake City*, Vol. II, (W. Jeffs, London), 1861, pp. 475–476.

guns. As I write this there are at least six heavy loaded revolvers in the tent besides bowie knives and other arms."[2]

Yet the dangers from the criminal element in the southland were as nothing compared to the troubles which mother nature visited upon the region during these years. In 1861–62 a tremendous series of rains flooded the region and wrecked havoc upon buildings, livestock and agriculture. The rains were followed by two terrible years of drought in which thousands of animals starved to death and the cattle industry, which had been the most important economic factor in the entire southland, virtually came to an end. This in turn led to foreclosures on the great ranches of the area. And, if these misfortunes were not enough the entire territory was visited by a serious and distressing epidemic of small pox which lasted for several years.

Still, culture of a kind and music as part of this culture did come to southern California and to Los Angeles. In this respect those who loved the finer things in life were no different than others before them who had helped to inhabit a thousand different places on America's ever-changing frontier. There have always been some who have demanded and have insisted upon the very best that an environment and a civilization could give. Before the time of which we speak—music in Southern California had been largely confined to mission and the ranchos. The mission choirs and crude orchestras had been composed of Indians—the rancho music consisted largely of that which accompanied a festival or a ball. At times, the firemen of the town sponsored a picnic in the Arroyo Seco, or someone sang in the program attendant upon a Washington's Birthday or Fourth of July celebration.

But, beginning with the 60's, music teachers began to come to southern California. As one might expect, most of them were German in nationality. And we begin to find cards like this one appearing in the one Los Angeles newspaper, *The Star*: "The undersigned has the honor to announce to the public that he has established a MUSIC CLUB, under the name of The Los Angeles Music Verein the object of which is to improve music in every respect." "The well known Musician and Music Teacher, Mr. H. Kull, lately from San Francisco, has accepted the Directorship of said Club, under whose head all musical entertainments will be given." "Orders for music for parties will be received by me, and the talent supplied on all occasions. . . . "[3] Another gentleman was quite versatile. The card in the *Star* of August 30, 1861 for Adolphus Brunne read: "Music Teacher—Violin, flute, guitar, English, Spanish and German languages—Voice—Furnish music for Balls and Parties, etc."

I hope that you understand that I'm not all seeing and all knowing. As one gets older, you find that you know less. But what you do know you believe in very strongly.—**"Humanistic Education," Little Rock, 1979.**

---

[2] Brewer, William; *Up and Down California* (Yale University Press, New Haven), 1930, p. 14.
[3] Los Angeles *Star*, May 26, 1860.

188

Mr. Kull, and others who followed after him gave occasional programs in John Temple's Hall which was erected over a market in 1860. Compositions at first consisted entirely of vocal numbers—and were definitely of the sentimental type. Furthermore, those who participated were not helped to grow professionally by the reviewers present. Here is a typical notice describing a church service:

> We noted many faces which for grace, sensibility and beauty might lead a man away from his devotions to the Deity if it were not for his notorious disposition not to notice such things. The worst thing about it is that it gets worse when you reach the choir. Miss Florida Nichols possesses a soprano voice which would attract attention in any choir in the United States. . . . Miss Belle Mallard would be a great card in any choir and her notes are as fresh as a bird's. . . . To our surprise the last hymn proved to be set to the air of the prayer in the opera of Tampa and it was a delicious conclusion to very interesting services.[4]

In spite of their lack of knowledge of music—the newspaper editors did everything in their power to encourage the patronage and interest of the people in cultural endeavors. For instance, one editor speaks rather sadly of the poor attendance at a lecture on music (and I imagine that everyone in this room at one time or another has shared his feelings):

> We are sorry to say that Mr. Potter's lecture on music was not generally attended. This is not as it should be. Mr. Potter has rendered efficient aid in a number of concerts and entertainments that have been given in this city for various charitable purposes, and the public should have shown their appreciation of his talent and liberality by attending his lecture. We would suggest that those whom Mr. Potter has so frequently and successfully assisted in concerts and musical entertainments, assist that gentleman in a concert for his benefit.[5]

However, those who were interested in music labored on, not only in teaching and in presenting occasional concerts for the few who were interested, but also but in trying to advance their own standards.

But if a certain lethargy on the part of the average citizen was not enough to discourage our first music teachers—they had another disadvantage, in that it was most difficult to secure music and instruments from the east or from San Francisco. The first music store in Los Angeles together with a flourishing insurance business was opened in 1870. An agency for Chickering pianos was announced in 1873. One can gather that interest in music grew slowly when the county assessor in 1872 listed in all of Los Angeles County only 114 musical instruments.

With such scanty resources Los Angeles musicians found it necessary to draw upon all available talent for the presentation of a formal

---

[4] Los Angeles *Express,* March 22, 1875.
[5] Los Angeles *News,* Nov. 20, 1866.

concert. A program typical of the period was that arranged for the congregation of the Jewish Synagogue. There were listed as entertainers eight of the local musicians supported by the entire company of the San Francisco Minstrels and by Professor Bosco, a magician. Included in the program were arias from *Robert Le Diable, Der Freischutz* and *Norma,* the Zampa overture, Mendelssohn leider and popular ballads. And since the minstrels had been generous with their talent, the Jews in the city returned the compliment and gave them a "benefit" several evenings later.[6]

The custom of giving a "benefit" was a great institution. Perhaps we should revive this very pleasant and sincere gesture in our busy and thoughtless twentieth century. Los Angeles musicians prospered according to the times. When money was scarce or when funds were desperately needed for some emergency, a benefit was the answer. Usually the affair was preceded by a public announcement such as this one in 1873:

> Los Angeles, Feb. 15th, 1873
>
> Mrs. Carl von Gulpen—Dear Madam:
>
> Learning that you are obliged to undertake an expensive journey for the improvement of the health of one of your children, we deem it highly proper on this occasion to express to you in a substantial manner our estimate of your uniformly kind courtesy in aiding by your distinguished musical services whatever benevolent enterprise has from time to time sought your assistance. We propose, therefore, to tender to you the benefit of a Concert, to be given at such a time and place as may best suit your convenience.[7]

The invitation bore the signatures of thirty prominent businessmen. A reply to the invitation always was couched in language which indicated "great surprise" on the part of the recipient:

> Los Angeles, Feb. 18th, 1873
>
> Messrs. John G. Downey, J. R. Toberman, J. Morehaut, and others:
>
> Gentlemen: Allow me most gratefully to acknowledge your very considerate offer of a Benefit. Although unexpected, your very kind intentions are truly appreciated by me, and I shall try, in company with some gifted musical friends, to merit a continuance of your friendly regards by rendering the proposed entertainment as attractive as possible. I name Tuesday, March 6th, as the time, and the Merced Theater as the place for holding such a Concert.[8]
>
> Very respectfully, Pauline von Gulpen

Very slowly in the early 70's opportunities for musicians and for music makers began to improve in southern California. In 1876 a railroad joined us with San Francisco. A whole series of seasonal fairs—

---

[6] Los Angeles *News,* June 4, 1869.

[7] Los Angeles *News,* Feb. 15, 1873.

[8] Los Angeles *News,* Feb. 18, 1873.

Flower Fairs, Chrysanthemum Fairs, Horticultural Fairs and Agricultural Fairs called forth the services of musicians. St. Vincent's College, now Loyola University, opened its doors in 1869 and shortly thereafter added music to its curriculum. The University of Southern California was to come along a bit later in 1881. Churches were founded, built imposingly and installed fine organs. A Philharmonics Society, after several abortive attempts finally got started in 1878. Los Angeles heard her first opera in 1874 and revelled in a homemade performance of "Pinafore" in 1879. The sentimental ballads were succeeded now and then by compositions of Schubert and Verdi, and Haydn and Beethoven were sung at St. Vibiana's Cathedral. The little German-English School sponsored a string quartet. But as the town and the county grew, there came into being the inevitable problem of rivalries, incompetency, and some suspicion.

The story of the growth of music in southern California is a fascinating one. And, no matter what year or period and in spite of discouragement, of economic or professional adversity, the result was always the same: eventual success for the musician who was talented and well trained, and who possessed standards above reproach. I could ask only that you and I be considered worthy to continue a musical tradition which was established so humbly and yet so firmly and magnificently by these predecessors of ours in California.

Appendix

The Writings
of Howard Swan

(A) Works Newly Published in this Compilation

"A Listener's Report on European Music: Implications for Americans," 1963.

"A New Program for Church Music," a lecture at the national convention of the American Guild of Organists, Pasadena, California, July 1962.

"Choral Tradition and the Choral Sound," Faculty Award Lecture, Occidental College, Los Angeles, California, October 17, 1966.

"Johann Sebastian Bach: Humanitarian, Musician, Theologian," an address, the First United Methodist Church, Pasadena, California, April 1, 1979.

"Music Teaching in Southern California 100 Years Ago," a talk, Los Angeles Chapter of the National Association of Teachers of Singing.

"Relationships Between Choirmaster and Clergyman," a lecture at Southern California Theological Seminary, October 12, 1960.

"Report to the Profession," an address, national convention, American Choral Directors Association, Dallas, Texas, 1977.

"The Choral Musician in a Changing World," commencement address, Westminster Choir College, May 20, 1977. Published in the *Westminster Choir College Newsletter,* June 1977. Used by permission.

"The Creed of a Chorister," an address at Pasadena Presbyterian Church, June 10, 1945.

"Three "T's" for Choral Success," unpublished paper.

"Why Art?" an address at the Plymouth Congregational Church, Des Moines, Iowa, April 1985.

(B) Writings Reprinted Wholly or in Part

The publisher is grateful to the following sources for their permission to reprint these articles.

"Los Angeles: American City," *The New Grove's Dictionary of Music and Musicians,* Volume 11, Sadie (ed.), London: MacMillan, Ltd., 1980.

"Musical Sounds for the Seventies—Safe, Subversive or Splendid?" address, general session, Arizona Music Educators Association Convention, published in *Arizona Music News,* (Volume 14, Number 2) December 1969.

"The Importance of the Personal Equation," *The Choral Journal,* October 1972.

"The Interpretation and Performance of Classic and Romantic Choral Music—A Practical Approach," a lecture for the institute of the Southern California Vocal Association, Herrick Memorial Chapel, Occidental College, October 1970. Monograph (Volume 4, Number 1), Southern California Vocal Association, 1970.

"The 'Lost' Art of Inspiration," *The Journal of Choral Conductor's Guild,* September/October 1968 (Volume 30 No. 1). Published in *The Choral Journal,* January/February 1969, and reprinted in the April 1986 issue.

"The Making of the Presidents, 1979," an address, Leadership Retreat, Lawton, Oklahoma, American Choral Directors Association, 1979. Published in *The Choral Journal,* May 1980.

"Steps to Choral Excellence: Choices, Compromises and Decisions," opening address, western division convention, American Choral Directors Association, San Diego, California, 1980. Published in two parts in the ACDA *Newsletter,* (Volume 8, Number 1) October 1981 and the following issue.

"Style, Performance Practice and Choral Tone," *CMEA News,* November/December 1965.

"The First American Performance of *La Boheme*," commentary, *Pioneer Western Playbills,* Number Eight, published by The Book Club of California, San Francisco, 1951.

"The Music of the Mormons, 1830-186," *The Huntington Library Quarterly* (Volume 12, Number 3) May 1949.

(C) Quoted Works

"Address," Western Division convention of the American Choral Directors Association, Pasadena, California, 1982.

"A Question of Balance," unpublished commencement address, Occidental College, June 14, 1986.

"Choice, Compromise, Courage, Confidence: A Choral Credo for the '80s . . . " Keynote Address, convention, Minnesota American Choral Directors Association, St. Cloud State University, published in *The Star of the North,* April 1981.

"Guest Editorial," *The Choral Journal,* March 1972.

"Humanistic Education," an address to administrators of the Pulaski County Special School District, Little Rock Arkansas, February 22, 1979.

"Keynote Address—TMEA 1985," *Southwestern Musician—Texas Music Educator,* May 1985.

"Objectives For a Choir," quotations by Swan excerpted from a thesis by Carole J. Glenn, *The Choral Journal,* November 1971.

"Recollections," (regarding Robert Shaw), *The Choral Journal,* April 1986.

"Symposium Summary, Observations and Reflections," an address, Texas Music Educators Association Symposium, June 11, 1977, published in the *Southwestern Musician,* December 1977.

"The Editor Interviews . . . Howard Swan," *The Journal of Choral Conductors Guild,* (Volume 31, Number 6) February 1970.

"The Nashville Symposium: 'A Cause for Celebration,'" (with Robert Shaw), *The Choral Journal,* October 1983.

"What Shall We Do with Church Music?" an unpublished address, University of Redlands, 1956.

D) Other Writings

"The Development of a Choral Instrument." In Decker, Harold A. and Julius Herford (eds.) *Choral Conducting, A Symposium.* Englewood Cliffs, New Jersey: Prentice-Hall, Inc., 1973.

"Foreword" to Helmuth Rilling, *Johann Sebastian Bach's B Minor Mass.* Princeton, New Jersey: Prestige Publications, Inc., 1984.

"Making Choices," guest editorial, *Update for Church Musicians,* (Volume 4, Number 1), Winter 1984, Hinshaw Music.

Interviews
and Writings
About Howard Swan

Bartels, William H., "Problems of Choral Interpretation and Technique," *The Choral Journal,* September 1972.

Bradt, David, "Chorale Conductor Lives Positively," *Daily Titan,* (Volume 15, Number 35), published by California State University at Fullerton, December 6, 1972.

Erney, C. T., "The Music and the Maestro," in *New Worlds* (Newport Beach, California: The Irvine Company), (Volume 4, Number 4), July/August 1973.

Glenn, Carole, "In Quest of Answers," *The Choral Journal,* November 1974. This article was excerpted from her thesis *Choral Practices in the United States,* Occidental College, Los Angeles, 1971.

McEwen, Douglas, *Music Philosophies, Choral Concepts, and Choral Techniques Employed by Selected Choral Conductors in Southern California Four-Year Colleges and Universities.* Doctoral Dissertation, Colorado State College, 1961.

Rassmussen, David, *Howard Swan, Teacher Conductor.* Doctoral dissertation in progress, Arizona State University, 198–.

Salisbury, Ann, "Dr. Swan Is Ready for His Swan Song," *Glendale News-Press,* Glendale, California, June 14, 1971.

Wetenkamp, Herb, "Three Models Deserving Emulation," *Continuum,* (Volume 6, Number 3), published by California State University at Fullerton, March 1977.

Whitman, Louise B., "A Founding Father: Howard Swan," *The Journal of Choral Conductor's Guild,* January/February 1985.

DATE DUE

FEB 1 5 89			
ILL 7111110			
FEB 6 '90			
MAY 3 1 '90			
IL 53646436 sent 090430 due 090611			
	261-2500		Printed in USA